Poe Motion

West Midlands Vol III

Edited by Steve Twelvetree

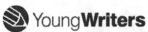 Young**Writers**
First published in Great Britain in 2004 by:
Young Writers
Remus House
Coltsfoot Drive
Peterborough
PE2 9JX
Telephone: 01733 890066
Website: www.youngwriters.co.uk

SB ISBN 1 84460 419 5

Foreword

This year, the Young Writers' 'Poetry In Motion' competition proudly presents a showcase of the best poetic talent selected from over 40,000 up-and-coming writers nationwide.

Young Writers was established in 1991 to promote the reading and writing of poetry within schools and to the youth of today. Our books nurture and inspire confidence in the ability of young writers and provide a snapshot of poems written in schools and at home by budding poets of the future.

The thought effort, imagination and hard work put into each poem impressed us all and the task of selecting poems was a difficult but nevertheless enjoyable experience.

We hope you are as pleased as we are with the final selection and that you and your family continue to be entertained with *Poetry In Motion West Midlands Vol III* for many years to come.

Contents

Khristian Beckett (11)	21
Aaron Patel (11)	21
Priyanka Patel (12)	22
Sheraan Rashad (11)	22
Laura Aston (12)	23
Courtney Young (12)	23
Joshim Ali (12)	24
Avtar Singh (12)	24
Zoheel Tariq (12)	25
Louie Gannon (12)	25
Joel Hunt (12)	26
Christopher Webster (13)	26
Amanda Myatt (12)	27
Catherine Albutt (12)	27
Hassan Sarwar (11)	28
Jovan Davis (12)	28
Becky Follows (13)	29
Aftab Chaudhry (11)	29
Tasin Dad (14)	30
Tara Janjua (12)	30
Priyanka Chauhan (12)	31
Kim Secker (12)	31
Haaris Hayat (11)	32
Sohila Grewal (12)	33
David Evans (13)	33
Emma Poole (13)	34
Jessica Smith (12)	34
Sukhminder Aulakh (14)	35
Mohammed Irfaan (14)	35
Sonum Razaq (13)	36
Trevor Beardmore (13)	36
Ross G Wilkinson (14)	37
Andrew Dowling (13)	37
Jacquelynne Baker (13)	38
Arjun Bhanot (13)	39
Sunil Patel (13)	39
Natalie Battisson (13)	40
Roheel Rashid (13)	40
Samuel Cash (13)	41
Katie Foster (14)	41
Stacey Alpine (13)	42
Edona Cani (13)	42

Arthur Terry School

Jodie Varley (14)   69
Rebecca Humphreys (14)   70
Vicky Clifford (14)   71
Robert Tipping (14)   72
Jessica Faulkner (11)   72
Stephanie Marie Malin (11)   73
Hannah Crowther (11)   74
Francesca Carnell (11)   75
Leanne Smewing (11)   75
Sophie Ward (11)   76
Jenny Palmer (11)   76
Matthew Perry (11)   77
George Cutler (11)   77
Matthew Eades (11)   78
Jade Tubb (11)   79
Sebastian Thornton (11)   80
Philippa Ward (11)   81
Ellen Furley (11)   81
Cherelle Leach (12)   82
Lee Turner (11)   83
Stephanie Evans (11)   83
Heather Lowe (11)   84
Christopher Gerald (11)   85
Hayley Humphries (11)   86
Mia Wright (11)   87
Lucy Hipkiss (11)   87

Bishop Vesey's Grammar School

Paul Abbotts (12)   88
Adam Brownhill (12)   88
Matthew Robinson (12)   89
Nikesh Pokar (12)   90
Aaron Morris (12)   90
Tom Hurst (12)   91
Richard Kelly (12)   92
Habib-Ur-Rehman (12)   93
Daniel Pryor (12)   94
Alex Dalley (12)   94
Sam Griffiths (12)   95
Josh Storer (12)   96
Andrew Marlow (12)   97

Bishop Walsh RC School

Broadway School (Sixth Form)

Codsall Community High School

Darlaston Community Science College

Deansfield High School

Chaumét Kenton (13)	168
Laura Pitt (12)	168
Leigh Thomas (13)	169
Stacey Williams (13)	170
Guisseppi Silba (11)	171
Autumn Anderson (13)	172
Simone Campbell (13)	173
Sara Thompson (14)	174
Adam Ajchinger (13)	175
Nichola Patrick (13)	176
Letish Fisher (13)	177
Richard Burns (14)	178
Daniel Whittaker (13)	179
Claire Lane (13)	180
Michayla Mallinson (13)	181
Joanne Johnson (11)	182

Hagley Middle School

Katie Weston (11)	182
Charles Hughes (12)	183
Matthew Wood (11)	183
Rebecca Priest (11)	184

King Edward VI College

Shellyane Bryan (16)	184
Lucinda Russell (16)	185
Dale Kedwards (16)	186
Kerry Pinches (16)	187
Caroline Davis (16)	188
Sarah Hazelwood (16)	189
Joe Stone (16)	189
Josie Adams (17)	190
Sophie Wythes (16)	190
Claire Lewis (16)	191
Sophie Gower (16)	191
Carly Snead (16)	192
Stacey Davies (16)	193
Jack Del-Vecchio (17)	194
Sam Brett (16)	195

The Poems

Heaven

I wonder what it's like up there,
have you ever wondered?
High up in the sky,
well have you?

There's angels and clouds,
drifting all around you.
Wherever you look there's smoky clouds,
there's nothing else but *you.*

You look around for somebody,
but realise you're the only one.
You try to move around,
when you suddenly hear a sound.

It's walking towards you,
you're in Heaven.
Oh my gosh, I know who it is,
it's God!

I wonder what it's like up there,
have you ever wondered?
High up in the sky,
well have you?

Minakshi Neelam Samrai (13)

The Talking Chalk!

Unfortunately, Mrs Beckworth is my teacher,
She is a nasty, horrible, cruel creature.
My story begins in a boring lesson,
Which took a quarter of my afternoon session.
I was sitting at the back of the class,
As we were singing so high we broke the glass.
Mrs Beckworth wrote on the blackboard,
Until my pupils drooped and loudly I snored.
I opened my eyes and saw a white piece of chalk,
It started to dance, walk and talk.
How weird I thought as I looked at it dancing,
Flip-flopping, somersaulting, francing and prancing.
'Hey you!' it said in a very rude manner,
Swinging on the top of our classroom banner,
Which said, *'Treat others as you would like to be treated yourself'.*
'You should read what you're sitting on,' I said, like an elf.
'You what?' it said, 'I can't hear you, you're dumb!'
'Which way?' I said, 'Can't speak or can't do a sum?'
'Can't do a sum,' it said, while drawing a big treble clef,
'But if you can't hear me, you must be deaf!'
'Shut up!' it shouted, 'Shut up!' I cried,
Until I was so hot, I felt I was being fried.
I kept on saying, shut up again and again,
Till the chalk's voice didn't sound like any old men.
It was Mrs Beckworth saying, 'Certainly dear!'
I was so hot I was in pain of saying, 'See ya!'
But the bell rang signalling the end of school,
As I packed my bag and heard the chalk saying,
'Ain't it cool!'

Saiesha Mistry (11)

Why?

Why is the world miserable?
Why is the world scared?
Why can't it be repaired?

Why is there a war?
Why can't it be stopped?
Can't you see we don't want to fight anymore?

People have to suffer
For your mistake,
Please stop, lives are at stake.

Why can't there be world peace?
Why can't you see?
The world is falling apart,
Because of you and me.

They never had any choice
To go to war
Children are frightened
Children have no homes to live in.

People are dirty
People are filthy
People are dying
People are crying
But we are still fighting.

Children have no food
But most of all, children have no families
Because we have killed them all.

Why can't we stop it?
Can't you see
You and me
Are making this world
A horrible place to be.

Siobhan Thompson (13)

I Want To Be The One . . .

I want to be the one who makes a difference,
I want to be the one who stops the pain,
I want to be the one who stops the hunger,
It's driving me insane.

I feel so strong about the war and poverty,
What happens to them all, it hurts to think,
Deep inside I can't ignore my feelings,
It's making my heart sink.

It's like no one cares about these people,
I'm going to visit places in despair,
Places without food and short of water,
I think it's so unfair.

I want to be the one who makes a difference,
I want to be the one who gets things done,
I want to be the one who stops the hunger,
I want to be the one.

Emma Clift (12)

The Loony In The Lavoisier Lab

Dreaming and talking with the gift of the gab,
Sitting and staring into space,
With an interested look on her face!

She'll chat to you for a little while,
Then turn and ask, 'Where's my file?'
She is in her own world that woman is,
Wonder how the kids can call her Mizz.

I'll never know how she became a teacher,
The interviewer must have been a really odd creature,
Probably from the same planet, I think,
Jupiter or Mars, now that's got to be the link.

Neelam Hussain (12)

Bloodstained Tears

You stole it from me,
All I ever had was in you.
My innocence was shredded
Like a paper doll,
I was cut with scissors
And now I cry
Bloodstained tears.

I can hear you whisper
Those lies, those words are like razors.
A poison of bittersweet memories
That we share
And now all that's left are my
Bloodstained tears.

I sit and wait,
My wrists slashed with a weapon of love.
And hate creeps into my veins,
Crawls out of the darkness
And into my dreams
So now all I cry is
Bloodstained tears.

In the end,
You stole my heart.
And soulless I was,
Until faith restored and love behold
Something to save me from myself
But still I cry
Bloodstained tears.

Cheryl Adcock (16)
Alderbrook School

My Dad

My dad . . .
A million stars . . .
A big, comfy bear . . .

Who held me tight . . .
And loved me from his heart . . .
A big cushion . . .

A sun . . .
That always shines on me . . .
The morning birds singing . . .

My dad . . .
My love.

Henna Zahoor (12)
Alderbrook School

Swimming

I like going swimming on a Sunday
Because it is a fun day.

At swimming I play with a ball
Which I throw against the wall.

I dive into the pool
Which is very cool.

I win the gold
Even though the water is cold.

Samina Mahmood (11)
Alumwell Business & Enterprise College

A Teacher's Nonsense Poem

I went to school with a bunch of keys,
My teacher saw them and started to sneeze.

When I put them down,
She pulled a face
Then started to frown,
But when I picked them up,
She ran away with a cup.

The class thought it was funny,
When the weather changed and it was sunny.

When I put the keys in my pocket,
My teacher was coming out of the socket.

I said to her that I was sorry,
She replied and said you don't need to worry.

I gave my teacher a great big hug,
She said to me, 'You are a lovely little bug.'

Afreen-Wajid Hussain (12)
Alumwell Business & Enterprise College

My Room

I like my bedroom, I like it loads,
I can change it to different modes,
When the moon rises,
My room is full of surprises,
Like the skeleton that glows in the dark.

When I wake up, my diary starts its writing,
My teddies start fighting
And I'm sick of that stupid cat
That sits on my mat,
Crying for more and more
I give him his food
And then I get booed
And he is still screaming for more.

Charli Aston (12)
Alumwell Business & Enterprise College

The Tiger

As the tiger lay in the grass
An antelope started to pass,
He scrunched up his eyes
And thought, *say your bye-byes*
And ran like a broken piece of glass.

He dashed in the heat,
So hungry for meat,
Then another one ran by
That he caught from his eye
And thought, *you can also say your bye-byes.*

After the tiger finished eating
He thought it was like having central heating
He went to get some water
And saw a cub pounce that he taught her
And thought, *that's not how you pounce, oh daughter!*

The tiger lay out of sight
And thought, *I'll have another bite*
He lay there in silence
And thought, *I'm getting a little high tense*
And went because it was nearly night.

Lucy Gartshore (11)
Alumwell Business & Enterprise College

The Classroom

In the classroom where I work,
There are folders that shout out to me,
The books start looking at me,
The pens start jumping
And the chairs walk up to me,
Books start to fly
And I get dizzy.

Siobhan Hodgetts (12)
Alumwell Business & Enterprise College

It's A Girl Thing

When girls get up in the morning,
Their faces are sleepy and boring.

Quickly get your toothbrushes,
To get ready your boy crushes.

Hurry up and get changed,
Then you will get a better boy range.

Do your hair all nice and neat,
Then you will find a guy named Pete.

Don't rush your make-up,
Because you will mess your face up.

It's time to go to school,
So just act cool!

Chetna Patel (12)
Alumwell Business & Enterprise College

Moon Magic

I went to bed last night to sleep
And out of the window my eyes did peep.
The stars were shining so happy and gay
The moon was glistening, like a winter's day.
Into the darkness my eyes did stare
The man on the moon just sitting there.
Morning approaching very fast
The thought of going to sleep at last.
It's time for bed, the sandman has been
We'll sit on the moon, like a king and a queen.

Rieanne Stuckey (12)
Alumwell Business & Enterprise College

The Bear

Beware the bear
With the shaggy hair.
If you go to the fair
You'll see his lair.

If you hear him at night
He just cries and cries,
Because he wants a friend
Before he dies.

They whip him and beat him
And hit him with bricks
Just to make him
Do silly tricks.

When they hit him
It's really cruel,
But other people laugh
And think it's cool.

When you hear him cry
It's like the sound of a lorry,
But when you see him
You'll feel sorry.

Faizel Patel (13)
Alumwell Business & Enterprise College

Winter

The crunching leaves
twirling around by the windowpane,
then slowly dropping on the soft ground.
Flowers dying in the cold wind.
Birds in tall trees desperately trying to keep warm.
People covering themselves
in gloves, hats, scarves and warm coats.
Winter is coming.

Bina Patel (12)
Alumwell Business & Enterprise College

Fog

Fog was coming everywhere
With no courage and no care,
It went everywhere near a shop
It went from the bottom to the top,
Nobody could make it stop
It went *bang, crack, bong, pop!*

It went everywhere even near here
It had no courage and no fear,
Everyone was scared, even me
The fog had no destiny,
Then I saw a man with a beard
Then the fog disappeared.

Jonathan Tonkinson (12)
Alumwell Business & Enterprise College

Life Itself

You never know where you stand,
In crowd, out crowd, find out first hand,
When life decides to put you down,
For the rest of the world you smile and wear a crown,
Pretending everything's OK,
You look down and walk away,
But inside you feel bruised,
Feeling like you're being used,
Your mind is playing tricks on you,
You feel a fool for all you do,
Like the world, without what seems, an end,
Or a not nice dream, let's play pretend.

Vicky Read (12)
Alumwell Business & Enterprise College

My Dream Island

My dream island is a place of peace
A place of joy and of fun,
With the glistening sea against the shore
And the sand so golden, I am so very sure.

A place where animals could roam free,
Along with others and of course me.
There would be no law or any crime
Just lots of people having a good time.

A tranquil island a place to go,
If you are wound up and feeling low,
When it's time to go
Trust me you won't want to go.

I would hold fun days,
Mondays, Fridays and Sundays,
Swimming, ball and croquet
I hope this becomes real someday!

Emma Greene (12)
Alumwell Business & Enterprise College

Problems

Problems, problems,
Never go away,
They're always there throughout the day,
There's too many bills you've got to pay.

You have many problems throughout the day.

Children, bills problems, are all,
You will end up with problems piled tall,
Get them sorted before they sort you,
Then your children will be happy and you will be too.

Amanda Dowling (12)
Alumwell Business & Enterprise College

An Aeroplane In Flight

It gets ready to take off
Listen to the engine parts
Oh my God
He's getting ready to start.

It goes down the runway
It's now getting fast
It's like a fisherman
Getting ready to cast.

It lifts up its nose
And then the rear
It tucks in its wheels
It's no longer near.

It does some loops
It flies upside down
It does some twirls
And then it goes round and round.

Its wings are like an eagle's
It's like a bird in flight
Making its mark in the clouds
I could watch it all night.

Lee Richard Holland (13)
Alumwell Business & Enterprise College

Winter

Winter is coming
The nights are getting dark,
There's no more playing out
Or visiting the park.

So all we've got to do
Is wait inside and play
And hope that Father Christmas
Will bring that special day.

Emma Aston (12)
Alumwell Business & Enterprise College

Supply Teacher

Here is the rule for what to do,
Whenever your teacher has the flu,
Or for some other reason takes to her bed
And a different teacher comes instead.

When this visiting teacher hangs up her hat,
Writes the date on the board, does this or that,
Always remember, you must say this,
'Our teacher never does that Miss!'

When you want to change places or wander about,
Or feel like getting the guinea pig out,
Never forget, the message is this:
'Our teacher always lets us Miss!'

Then, when your teacher returns the next day
And complains about the paint or clay,
Remember these words, you just say this,
'That other teacher told us to Miss!'

Sadia Kauser (12)
Alumwell Business & Enterprise College

Life

It is exactly the same but completely different,
It is as black as coal but as white as snow,
It is as hot as the sun but as cold as ice,
It is as bright as a torch but as dark as the night,
It is as dry as the Sahara but as wet as rain,
It is as alive as man but as dead as a dodo,
It is as blunt as a spoon but as sharp as a knife,
It is as small as an ant but as big as an elephant,
'What is this mysterious object?' I say to myself,
It is life.

Jagdeep Grewal (12)
Alumwell Business & Enterprise College

The Battle Of The Bulge

Bullets flying everywhere
What am I to do?
I'll pull out my gun
And aim it right at you.

I'll take careful aim now,
Looking down my sight.
Just pull the trigger,
I'll surely win the fight.

Bang, bang, bang,
They're all dead.
I must have shot them
All in the head.

Nooooo!
They have stormed the trench
I have to hide,
Under the bench.

They are so close,
They're coming nearer
I value my life,
So much dearer.

Bang . . . bang . . .
I have been shot
I am just alive
But not a lot.

Oh no,
It's turning white
I surely must have
Lost the fight . . .

Dafydd Evans (12)
Alumwell Business & Enterprise College

The Happy Sunday Has Arrived!

It was Monday,
But I was waiting for Sunday.
The reason why I hate Monday,
Is because it is never a fun day.

Usually, Tuesdays fly with flying colours,
But today it was colourless,
To make it right,
Time should fly tonight.

If the days could go so fast,
I believe I could last.

Wednesday has started, what should I do?
Maybe today I'll have fun,
I guess not, it's still dull.

Thursday has started with a rainy day,
With all the raindrops on the ground,
What's the use of doing anything?

Why does every second of my life go so slow, is it natural?

I guess you know Friday has rised,
I'm amazed I haven't sized.
The rain has stopped and the snow has started
And today is the day to have some fun
But I better do as I'm told,
Cos Mummy says I can't catch a cold.

A little sun shines on my face on Saturday,
I hope I can last to see Sunday.

What should I do in the last minute of the dreadful week?
Maybe sing until Sunday is deep with sunshine and fun.

Yes, Sunday is finally here, here!
Time to play on the computer,
But wait, the sun has come out,
I guess it's really time to play outside, on the slide.

Monday has started all over again,
What should I do this time?
Maybe this time, I'll go to the land of happiness.

Lisa Chauhan (12)
Alumwell Business & Enterprise College

Complaint

The teachers all sit in the staffroom
The teachers all drink tea
The teachers all smoke cigarettes
As cosy as can be.

We have to go out at playtime
Unless we bring a note
Or it's tipping down with rain
Or we haven't got a coat.

We have to go out at playtime
Whether we like it or not
And freeze to death if it's freezing
And boil to death if it's not.

The teachers can sit in the staffroom
And have a cosy chat
We have to go out at playtime,
Where's the fairness in that?
Oh no!

Natalie Lycett (12)
Alumwell Business & Enterprise College

The Race

He's racing now,
The crowd's going wild,
As his first place is near,
Just one curve to go,
He's swerved out of control,
Smack! Bang!
Oh God! He's hit the wall,
The paramedics are rushing to his aid,
Dodging and swerving out of the way,
Just to find out, it's a bit too late.

Pritesh Patel (13)
Alumwell Business & Enterprise College

What Is Poetry?

P is for poems that mean a lot
O is for the outstanding things poetry does
E is for enjoying poems
T is for true love that poems describe
R is for reading poems
Y is for your emotions.

M is for motions
O is for our poems
T is for things poems do
I is for I like poetry
O is for oh poetry is fun
N is for nothing is better than poetry.

Abdul Qaseem (12)
Alumwell Business & Enterprise College

The Ferrari

The Ferrari
Sounds like an army
Moving on the road,
It moves that fast,
You can't get past,
It is much faster than a toad,
The Ferrari
Swerves around the curve,
It is so fast,
You can't get past,
It really is a sports car.

Jenny Jones (13)
Alumwell Business & Enterprise College

Racism Abuse

As I walk down the street, I am scared that someone will torture me,
I go to the park, everyone's having fun.
Except me!
As I walk towards the swings, everybody *stops,*
Stares at me like a piece of junk on the floor.
They give me dirty looks,
They all whisper to each other as I approach them.
I can hear,
Heartbreaking words said to me.
I am so empty inside.
I feel like I am *nothing!*
Dead inside,
I pray to God to ask him, 'Please let at least one person be kind to me.'
But it doesn't happen!
I will commit suicide today, *hang myself,*
Torture myself.
I am nothing!

Daniel Sanghera (11)
Alumwell Business & Enterprise College

Hunny Bunny

She's lovely and she's gorgeous
She's mad and ever so funny
Always glad, she's never sad
Adorable hunny bunny.

Katrina Morrison (12)
Alumwell Business & Enterprise College

Arsenal Winning 7-1

As Arsenal are winning 7-1
Liverpool are rubbish says everyone
Henry 5, Pires 2
Liverpool are screaming we don't know what to do
Henry skipped past the keeper
Something caught his eye it was a streaker
He ran all around the football pitch
But in the end he fell in a ditch
The police came and took him away
But now Henry had to pay
Carragher came and slid in
He tackled him so hard he broke Henry's shin.

Patrick Gannon (11)
Alumwell Business & Enterprise College

Liverpool's Players

Michael Owen is the best
Jerzy Dudek always needs a rest,
Emile Heskey is the top scorer,
Sammi Hyypia is the class defender,
Liverpool are better than the rest.

Harry Kewell is always the man of the match,
Jamie Carragher is the one to snatch,
Diao is a mid,
Gerrard always skids.

Zaahid Isakjee (11)
Alumwell Business & Enterprise College

Patience

Patience is a virtue,
patience means to wait,
be patient
if your friends are late.

If in life you wait,
people will be devoted to you
and not hate.

Jesus waited all that day,
did he not?
And look what he got,
wait and you'll have your way.

People who have waited have done well in life,
they've been through worse
and gone through good.

Khristian Beckett (11)
Alumwell Business & Enterprise College

Liverpool FC

As he plays the ball to the keeper,
He notices the players get deeper.
The Arsenal players are losing 5-1,
The fans think it's a con.
Michael Owen has gone all the way,
He'd better score or he'll have to pay.
The fans are cheering as loud as they can.
One of the players has just got a one match ban.
Liverpool have won the game,
Looks like their luck really came.

Aaron Patel (11)
Alumwell Business & Enterprise College

Winter, Spring, Summer, Autumn

Winter is fun, the snow is just right
Bells ringing in the outdoor light,
Kids come and adults too,
Singing carols to all of you,
Spring, spring everywhere
Buds and flowers look like they stare,
The air is fresh, the trees bloom,
But the trees need lots more room.
Summer has come with a boiling sun,
Girls and boys just run and run.
Eating ice cream served ice-cold,
New trees replace the old.
Autumn is here, leaves there,
Red, gold, brown and yellow everywhere
Falling to the ground, round and round,
Together they are all bound.

Priyanka Patel (12)
Alumwell Business & Enterprise College

Boring Day

It's a very boring day,
Giants walking in the streets
Dragons flying in the sky.

It's a very boring day,
Cows jumping in the sky.
Lions knocking on the door for tax.
It's a very boring day,
Cats chasing people, like dogs.
Pigs flying in the sky with wings,
Babies rampaging in the streets
It's a very boring day,
Why doesn't the day just end?

Sheraan Rashad (11)
Alumwell Business & Enterprise College

The Weather's Way

Autumn windy, rather wet,
Summer, spring are the best.
The autumn colours, red, gold, brown
Leaves are dropping to the ground.

Winter weather is the worst,
Icicles are coming first.
Sitting with toast in front of the heater,
The money dropping in electric meter.

Spring is coming with fresh green leaves,
In the air and over seas,
The fresh air is smelling
And people are telling.

Summer is hot,
All the plants die in their pots.
Playing with water
Makes such a fine day.

Laura Aston (12)
Alumwell Business & Enterprise College

Leave Me Alone

Why do people bother me?
Just leave me alone peacefully.

Why do people constantly ask me what's wrong?
They know if I explained it would be too long.

So leave me alone and let me be,
Please just stop bothering me.

But there is something I would like to say,
It cheers me up playing sports every day.
Sports are in
My thoughts.

Courtney Young (12)
Alumwell Business & Enterprise College

My Dear Uncle

I have an uncle who acts like a clown,
who visits the markets but not the town,
he drives a red Mini
which is really cold and tiny.

His name is Ian, 'David Ian',
he hates my nan,
for a present gives her a pan,
but *luuuvs* his gran.

He was born in Australia,
moved to Canada,
lived in Florida,
Course he made that up, he stayed in Colombia.

Now he has run away,
because he stole an ashtray
and a big red belt buckle,
ladies and gentlemen, my dear uncle.

Joshim Ali (12)
Alumwell Business & Enterprise College

Sports Are For Life

Sports are made for life,
You can play them with your wife.

There are lots of sports such as basketball,
For this you should be tall.
You should be tall,
But it's alright to be small.

On one hand there is basketball,
On the other there's football.

They are very good sports,
They take a lot of thought.

Avtar Singh (12)
Alumwell Business & Enterprise College

The Uncool Fool

I was walking to school,
When I turned the corner, I saw a fool,
I was kicking a can,
It landed on the fool called Tan.
He thought he was cool,
But I thought he was uncool.
He followed me down the road
With a lead and a black toad.
He carried on down,
Said he was going to town.
He has a red mini
That is really tiny.
It is a 3-wheeler.
He was wearing a red hat,
That had a picture that looked like a bat.
He followed me straight through the school gate,
Then I found out that I was late.
He started to pump me,
I gave him a lump.
After that I never saw him again.

Zoheel Tariq (12)
Alumwell Business & Enterprise College

My Bright Star

You can't see them during the day,
twinkling at night,
I wish I could be up there
and see them so bright,
I'd hold them so tight
and never let them go,
as I am down low
and you are up high,
shining in the sky.
In the dark night
you hold me from fright.

Louie Gannon (12)
Alumwell Business & Enterprise College

The Road

The road goes past mountains and hills,
Whether you travel by foot or wheels,
The road is long and never ends,
Around a corner and some bends.

The road never ends, it never stops,
Over the river and climb some rocks,
Some badgers meet me and a fox,
I pass a farmer and his crops.

When will I get there? When will I rest?
Up, down, up, down goes my chest,
I see my house, it is not far.

The homely chairs, the blazing fire.

Sing, 'Hey!' for my heart is beating,
The dinner in the oven, I am now fleeting,
A nice cup of tea would please me,
So I sit down and watch TV!

Joel Hunt (12)
Alumwell Business & Enterprise College

Respect Me As One

Black is the colour of my skin,
Not of my soul that lives within.
To be accepted as one,
An equal,
The same,
Will always be my goal,
My aim!
To live,
To love,
To be happy,
To live my life as one.
But I shouldn't have to try,
You should accept me *as one*.

Christopher Webster (13)
Alumwell Business & Enterprise College

The Midnight Stallion

The midnight stallion,
straight and tall,
Proudly looks
over my wall.

He gallops through
the moonlight sky,
And then I suddenly
hear him cry.

I quickly run
down the stairs,
Oh just look
at how he stares.

His dark brown eyes,
just glaring at me,
Oh you really,
really should see.

His skin shining
in the starry sky,
Now the night
has gone by.

Amanda Myatt (12)
Alumwell Business & Enterprise College

Hallowe'en

Moon is shining, stars are bright,
The ghosts will come out tonight.
Spooky, scary, horrid things
Which fly about without wings.

Trick or treaters walking around,
Waiting for treats to be found.
See the ghosts, they're on their way
Trick or treaters run away.

Now the ghosts have come out to play!

Catherine Albutt (12)
Alumwell Business & Enterprise College

About A War

Heads blown off
Legs chopped off
Hostages being held
Until they give news.

Machine guns being fired
And people going *boom!*
'Cover me now, soldier,
Move in, move in, move in!'

Boom, boom, boom!
Fire all weapons,
Crash, boom, kapow!
We are in Vietnam
Fighting for our country.

Hassan Sarwar (11)
Alumwell Business & Enterprise College

Danger Of Speed

The tornado has no limit in speed
But why does it hunt? What does it need?

A car, not natural but manmade,
Just as bad as a diamond-cut blade.

The cheetah has more speed than brains
But with great speed comes pain.

The gazelle more wise and swift
No need to hunt, just treasure this great gift,
Less speed increases life.

Jovan Davis (12)
Alumwell Business & Enterprise College

Moon And The Stars

The moon and the stars
shine brightly in the sky.
I'm wishing that I could
be up there and fly.

Because my head is filled
with love, love from the
moon and stars,
there is nothing more
exciting than reaching out
and finding a little star.
A star that's filled with love,
love for me and you.
Because together we will
pull through and through.

Through the hurt and the pain,
this is driving me insane.
Just to reach out and find
a star I can say is mine.

Becky Follows (13)
Alumwell Business & Enterprise College

Speeding

S uper cars are made for speeding
P owered by horse power engines,
E xhausts large enough to live in
E ngine as powerful as a stampede of elephants
D arting around too fast to take a look,
 I gnoring people, lights and posts,
N ever stops,
G laring lights.

Aftab Chaudhry (11)
Alumwell Business & Enterprise College

War Thoughts

I sat in my seat, thinking only war,
Knowing I was safe, behind the closed door.
The thought of the surroundings, making me wonder,
What might it have been like, listening to all the blunder?
The sight of all the guns, artillery and more,
What was all the madness being made reality for?
How could the soldiers, be living through the stench,
As they lay waiting, for some movement in the trench.
I've never imagined, what it would feel like to be,
As I've never left the warmth, of this classroom with me.
I can't reconstruct, the smells, sights or sounds,
I'll just leave it to my head, to picture the firing rounds.
The rough earth and dust, rubbing on fighters' faces,
Everyone squashed together, in the small, tight places.
But I'm in a safe, easy to live in area,
While the soldiers are being bitten, therefore catching malaria.
The taste of the air, must have been cold and bitter,
Not mentioning all the infections, caused by lice litter.
I'm just glad, that I wasn't born then,
But I feel commiseration, for all the lost men.
I just hope, that from now on starting today,
The world becomes war free, and that's how it should stay.

Tasin Dad (14)
Alumwell Business & Enterprise College

My Bedroom

My bed sleeps through the night
As my computer jumps, hitting the light.
My mirror sings, oh so sweet,
As my speakers walk with their big feet.
My wardrobe dances in a joyful mood,
As my CD player's talk is very rude.
My dressing table listens all around for a sound.
Finally I get to my door as it shuts behind me
And pushes me to the floor.

Tara Janjua (12)
Alumwell Business & Enterprise College

My Room

I woke up; I got out of my comfortable, cosy bed,
I stood upon the ground; the room was small, cold.
I walked along the cold ground; my feet were as cold as ice,
I opened the huge cupboard; I took out my warm clothes.
I combed my hair, put scrunchie bobbles in,
I opened the cream's lid, the cream was hard as rock.
I got out my pen and pencil, sat on my bed,
Doing my homework was giving me a headache.
I walked along the cold ground,
I got into my cosy bed,
I was thinking about something.
As the night was falling,
I fell asleep.

Priyanka Chauhan (12)
Alumwell Business & Enterprise College

Five Irish Boys

Their mouths chatter,
lights dance,
fans shatter,
pyrotechnics prance,
that's the effect of five Irish boys.

Hair jumps,
sound blasts,
you might get goosebumps,
you will last and last,
that's the effect of five Irish boys.

Kim Secker (12)
Alumwell Business & Enterprise College

School

Back of the classroom,
During a boring lecture,
I was yawning and snoring,
It was 9am,
The first day in school,
The first lesson in school.

I thought to myself,
How long till the holidays?
How long till I can play all day?
How long till I can sleep all day,
And how long till I can talk all day?

Now it was break
When I slept behind the bushes,
Snoring and talking in my sleep,
I almost missed my next lesson
But the gardener heard me snore and talk.

It was another boring lesson
Until the teacher let us have an extra break,
Lucky me, she didn't see me sleep,
Lucky me, she didn't hear me snore or talk.

But as I was walking out
She totally freaked me out
By jumping at the door
And saying the words that meant I was unlucky,
Unlucky me.

At last she let me out,
Outside I planned to run out of school
Through a hole in the fence
But then I realized,
The remaining lessons were maths and science.

Haaris Hayat (11)
Alumwell Business & Enterprise College

Kick-Boxing

As the punchbags sway
They get punched day by day,
The boxing gloves walk
And as they walk they talk,
Uniform fights,
While it's fights they get hit by the lights.
Helmets crash together
They even say,
'We will be here forever and ever.'
The mirrors stare
The fighters just glare,
Belts chatter,
When they sort each other out,
They clatter and clatter.

Sohila Grewal (12)
Alumwell Business & Enterprise College

Doom

The bombs are dropping, so are all the people,
the death of war to affect us all.
Guns boom as darkness glooms
as the shrapnel spreads
the human doom,
as the bombs
drop . . . the people stop
and think, *I'm doomed!*

David Evans (13)
Alumwell Business & Enterprise College

World War I

In our classroom it is warm and dry,
in the trenches it was cold and wet.
We are all fresh and clean,
they were lice-infested and had regrets.

In the classroom, it is bright,
in the trenches it was drab.
In the classroom it smells nice,
in the trenches it smelt bad.

In the classroom, it is safe and secure,
in the trenches it was dangerous.
In the classroom there are choices,
in the trenches nobody listened to voices.

Emma Poole (13)
Alumwell Business & Enterprise College

Winter

Winter appears each year,
December is the time of year.

It is the time when crystal snowflakes
take over the lakes.

And birds prepare for the snow to whoosh down
houses are covered in white snow
as high as the snow can go.

The animals grow their winter fur
and breathe in the perishing air.

Jessica Smith (12)
Alumwell Business & Enterprise College

Christmas

Christmas is a time,
For giving and sharing
With people who love you
And who are caring.

The dinner is magnificent,
It's a genuine feast
With lots of boiled vegetables
And different types of meat.

The presents are stacked
Neatly under the tree.
There's a present for you
And a present for me.

Carols are then sung
By families with glee.
One of my favourites is
'Oh Christmas Tree'.

Sukhminder Aulakh (14)
Alumwell Business & Enterprise College

Death Message

Death is what will come to us all
no matter what age, big or small.
Emotion we will feel and fear will come,
some will be scared and some act dumb.
Live your life as well as you can,
because you might just die, just like your nan.
Life is a gift that you don't want to waste,
live happily ever after, and head for big tastes.
Now you are yet young, you have a friend
for a laugh and a joke on him you depend.

Mohammed Irfaan (14)
Alumwell Business & Enterprise College

Love . . .

Love is fate
it always comes along,
find your soulmate,
you can never go wrong.

Love hurts,
hearts breaking,
piece by piece,
always aching.

Love has regrets
getting in the way,
but just take life as it comes,
take it day by day.

But true love is forever,
never going apart,
always together,
in each other's hearts.

Sonum Razaq (13)
Alumwell Business & Enterprise College

Learn Or Mourn

Our life is good,
They traipse through mud,
We sit on our school bench,
They're in a stinking trench.

We are in a clean, safe place,
They're in a filthy, confined space.
Whilst we are learning,
They are mourning.

At school the work is mundane,
In the trench, they're firing guns.

Trevor Beardmore (13)
Alumwell Business & Enterprise College

School Boy Soldier

Our life is good
The classroom is our space
Their life was in mud
The trenches were their base
We study for our future.

We dream of a sandy beach
And listen to church bells
They secure a breach
And wait for wailing shells
Many lost their future.

Ross G Wilkinson (14)
Alumwell Business & Enterprise College

Trench

Maths, history, geography and French,
This might be boring,
But nothing like a trench.

Dead bodies underneath me,
All covered in rot,
I'm so scared,
I was nearly shot.

In the trench it's all bloody and gory,
So don't think of school as boring.

Andrew Dowling (13)
Alumwell Business & Enterprise College

Studying Hell

Whilst working in class,
I saw friends in trenches,
I see death.
Classrooms were bright, open and airy,
Now in trenches I am weary,
As death is around the corner,
All I shall think of is home
And how I'm alone.

In class it smells of caretaker's bleach,
Perfume and daily smells of school,
In trenches it smells like rotten meat,
How I miss my homely treats,
In class I could go to school fresh,
In trenches I smell filthy.

I am killing but not for the thrill,
If I stand and shoot,
I'll ask myself why
Instead of being shot by the enemies,
I murder instead,
I could have one clean bullet . . .

Will God take me in?

I wish to die
And that's not telling a lie,
Please don't cry,
I'm in Heaven or Hell.

Jacquelynne Baker (13)
Alumwell Business & Enterprise College

Soldiers At War

Waiting, waiting, waiting,
To see if it's the end of your life,
Sweating, sweating, sweating,
Asking yourself, will I see my wife?

Cold, wet conditions,
Everyone together feeling claustrophobic,
Sitting without protection,
Smell of dead bodies, unhygienic.

People killing,
Dying in dirt,
Soldiers shooting,
While men get hurt.

Do not lose your concentration,
It may make you pay,
You may not see your family
Or the break of day.

Would I ever see my children or wife
Or would my family cry?
Would I wake up to another day of my life
Or get shot and be left to die?

Would other soldiers feel this way?
Just sitting there thinking,
Would I see the end of day?
Death's the cause of my heart sinking.

Arjun Bhanot (13)
Alumwell Business & Enterprise College

Death Warrant

I've seen so many people fly
Now all I want to do is die.

I saw my friend calmly walk by
And wondered, would he die?
A bullet came, it was goodbye!

Sunil Patel (13)
Alumwell Business & Enterprise College

I Have A Cat Called Shorty

I have a cat called Shorty,
Who is not forty,
He is really cute,
But he doesn't like fruit.

He likes cheese and meat
And has cute little feet,
He has a long tail
And he is male.

I love him so much,
His miaows are double-Dutch,
He is brown, black and white,
He's always in a fight.

He's got green eyes and whiskers too,
He doesn't say moo,
He lies on the chair,
He doesn't care.

I have a cat called Shorty,
Who is not forty,
He is really cute
But he doesn't like fruit.

Natalie Battisson (13)
Alumwell Business & Enterprise College

War

Filth here, filth there,
Soldiers being shot everywhere.
The smell of guts polluting the place
And when you get shot you fall on the floor.
You see the insides of people,
You die in an instant.

Roheel Rashid (13)
Alumwell Business & Enterprise College

Is School That Bad?

Double maths, history, chemistry and French,
All of these are good compared
To the terrors of the trench.

Rats and rodents, fleas and bites,
Ticks, diseases, mud and fights,
Wet and cold, hungry and bored,
Nothing to do till the cannons roared.

Dinners in detention, break on a bench,
Ha! This is nothing . . .
Just think about the stench!

So you may think that school's a bore,
Go on, laugh, but just think,
You wouldn't last a day in war.

Samuel Cash (13)
Alumwell Business & Enterprise College

Untitled

As I look out the classroom window,
I see the sun shine through,
I turn back around and listen to the teacher,
While I'm doing my work,
I think to myself how untidy it would be,
Without a teacher to put all the chairs,
Under tables and clean the boards,
Sometimes I smell the lovely smell,
Of girls' perfume and hairsprays,
I look at the cupboard, chairs and
Tables and can't see one bit of dust,
I feel safe in classrooms when
Teachers are there, they protect us from
The bullies!

Katie Foster (14)
Alumwell Business & Enterprise College

Life In The Trenches

The classroom is so different,
From the trenches in the war,
All the working in the class,
Is really such a bore!

But we take the class for granted,
We would have known long ago,
If we were in the war,
The cold would be our foe.

Inside the dirty trenches,
They lived, left loved ones behind,
They have no choice but to wait,
In the small space of mud, they're confined.

With hardly any food,
Only rations to survive,
Sitting, waiting amongst the dead
For the enemy to arrive.

But now back to the classroom,
All clean and safe,
Each one of us says a prayer,
For their bravery and sacrifice.

Stacey Alpine (13)
Alumwell Business & Enterprise College

Nightmares

I had a nightmare of flying on air,
I thought I was going to fall,
But no, I stayed up in the air.

I woke up in the morning
And thought I was flying
But then I fell down crying.

Edona Cani (13)
Alumwell Business & Enterprise College

War From A Classroom

We work in classrooms with our mates,
They lurk and wait, for the enemy to overtake,
In a classroom, there's a calm atmosphere,
In a trench, there's the smell of fear.

Classrooms, we have time to dream,
In a war, people scream,
Waiting, waiting, waiting they were,
While I was sitting there, talking to her.

When I'm with friends, I feel so secure,
Then there's the soldiers, who are alert and sure,
We have large spaces, and room to move,
They are cramped, squashed, dirty and alone.

We are happy, and warm in our classroom ,
Out there they are dangerous
And waiting to attack.

Cheryl Wiggin (14)
Alumwell Business & Enterprise College

Detention Vs Death

I'm stuck doing schoolwork and then getting more,
But at least I'm not leaving to fight a war,
I'm safe and warm so I'm not complaining,
I could be out in the trenches where it's cold and raining.

Essay and algebra it's all pretty grand,
Compared to being out in no-man's-land,
The teacher's voice I hardly hear,
But you can't ignore the sounds of pain and fear,
Outside I can see the shining sun,
But in war there's just blood and guns.

So in the end it's obvious to all,
I'd rather be in school with its high towering wall,
Then over the seas in foreign lands,
In the army's front line, among the first to fall.

Salma Tarajia (14)
Alumwell Business & Enterprise College

Class And War

War is what we are reading at school,
My vision of war is that I've been such a fool,
Reports, plays and stories is what we do,
Sometimes we put on voices too.

The trenches sound horrible,
Accounts sound improbable,
Guns and bombs galore,
Which the boys are all for.

A nice, clean, safe classroom,
No *bang, bang, boom, boom,*
Cherry blossom smells surround me,
Don't have to pay my life as a fee.

A fee for freedom, life and love,
What did they suffer, those soldiers up above?
As I sit in this classroom thinking of war,
I don't have to live with it anymore.

Amy Austin (13)
Alumwell Business & Enterprise College

Cars

In a car the wheels run,
The exhaust starts to smoke,
On the car the bonnet starts to talk,
On the car the door waves at passers-by,
The hand brake starts to jump,
In a car the gear box dances,
In the car, the horn shouts at crazy people.

Sam Harding (12)
Alumwell Business & Enterprise College

Life In The Trenches

In an uncomfortable trench we wait,
Our enemies lurk there, the people we hate,
In a comfortable classroom we're working,
There are no enemies lurking.

In trenches we're always ready,
Classrooms they take it steady,
The trenches smell of rotten flesh,
Our classroom smells lemon-fresh.

In the trenches, the environment's bad,
We miss our families we're all sad,
In the classroom the environment's nice,
The classrooms are clean, we don't get body lice.

The trenches are such a squeeze,
Send us home to our families please,
Our classroom has large spaces,
All around us are familiar faces.

In an uncomfortable trench we wait,
Our enemies lurk there, the people we hate,
In a comfortable classroom we're working,
There's no enemy lurking.

Carly Russon (13)
Alumwell Business & Enterprise College

Crashing For The Goal

Kicking the football up to the goal,
The ball is moving as fast as the wind,
It's a goal!
The people shout,
Kicking the ball and flying like pieces of coal,
Zigging and zagging, tackling and kick,
Speeding up to the wind,
Running, running round the pitch,
Speeding! Ready to crash for the goal.

The wind is whistling and blowing hard on my face,
The ball swishing and swashing at my lace,
It's started to rain,
The raindrops come down on me,
Like water has tipped on you.

The game is called off,
I could have made that goal.

Sophie Gartshore (11)
Alumwell Business & Enterprise College

Fierce Match

There was a silence
Both captains were looking
At each other angrily
The whistle had blown
They were ready to kick off
The ball began to speed
Legs started breaking
Fans started running
Players getting sent off
Net started falling
Everyone started fighting
Match getting abandoned
Managers getting annoyed.

Abdul Basith (12)
Alumwell Business & Enterprise College

Cars

I was in my car
Driving very far
My sunroof squeaked
At the people on the street,
I was honking my horn to
The people that I met,
The doors slammed and
The people were clamped,
I saw this man with the same car
But my car is the star!

Andrew Foster (12)
Alumwell Business & Enterprise College

Gone Forever

Do you remember when it was safe to play on the streets?
Do you remember when everyone was part of a community?
Do you remember life without the latest technology?
Do you remember the happiness of children's faces?
Do you remember when we had to walk miles for water?
Do you remember when teenagers weren't afraid to
                                    be seen with their parents?

Streets are not safe, many children are killed every year,
People keep themselves to themselves,
The word 'unsociable' now exists.
Life is now about mobile phones and the latest computer games,
Children have to deal with divorce of parents and death,
We have an easier life now, water is always there,
Teenagers are too involved with their friends,
Family is not always considered.

Amy Heise (15)
Arthur Terry School

Carpet Man

Escape
  Escape
    Escape

To anywhere if I could,
If only for a time, I would,
A desperate need for if I stay,
What will happen? Who can say?

Escape
  Escape
    Escape

In the back of a lorry or hold of a boat,
Perhaps make a raft and just hope that I float,
Amongst the oil, the swirls are my home,
My head's light like feather but my heart's like a stone.

        A carpet

A carpet man!
I know I can!
To a far-off land!
To a far-off land!

I shall roll myself up in a carpet or rug
And finish up wherever I finish up
And I'll live where I live and run through the rain,
As I build up a life, but then flee again.

From a war-torn country where persecution is shown,
I'll be a carpet man in a carpet home . . .

Amy Hextell (15)
Arthur Terry School

Poetry In Motion

Let me go
This is not right
My brain is going to explode
What shall I do?

What is the point of life?
Trapped in chains,
Never to see sunlight,
Never to feel happiness.

In the past,
It was like night was day
And day was night.

Coming out
Like a shadow in the dark,
Hiding in day like a bat.

Hiding in
Buildings,
Boxes,
Sewers,
Running slowly away from them.

'Rat get up, time for your execution.'

I am being taken
To death,
To the chair,
Get the wet sponge off my head,
What is this helmet doing?
This shall be my final day,
I want no more killing,
No more death.

Stephen Rogers (11)
Arthur Terry School

Don't Play With Rats

The morning was like a start of a new world, so nice,
But all this will stop 'Ah mice'
It could only be mom,
Every morning she explodes like a bomb,
I ran downstairs, dodging the cat,
When I was down, 'It's a rat,'
My mom was screaming and screaming,
Woke the neighbour, he was beaming,
Dad tripped over the floor,
But no one noticed the open door,
My dad's face was like hot chilli,
With me almost knocking over my brother Billy,
The rats ran through the open door,
Still running through, rough, wet floor,
I ran after them acting brave and bold,
But the only thing I caught was a cold,
Staying home wasn't so bad though,
But something was burrowing up inside, I had to go,
I ran out the back,
But suddenly I had an attack,
Something was crawling inside my belly,
It was like some kind of sticky, slimy, slithering jelly,
What are you doing? My mom got me some medicine,
As that kicked into gear,
My mom said, 'I guess it will be another week here,'
A whole week, why can't it be a day?
But whatever happens I'll find a way.

Mark Parsons (11)
Arthur Terry School

Gone Forever

My loved one has gone, we're no more together,
He's always in my heart and I'll love him forever,
When I felt the rain upon my back,
All I could remember, was the day of the attack.
It was a dark, stormy night, just like this,
The same very night, we had our last kiss.
The moon was bright and the shadows were getting near,
Little did we know about that evil fear.
The rain got harder, as if it was about to flood,
Swimming to the drains, his clean pure blood.
The evil knife struck upon his fair head
And I can never stop thinking of it, as I lay here in my bed,
I wake up in bed, still living in fear,
I know deep down, his heart will always be near,
His body lies peacefully six foot under
And I'll always have to stop and forever have to wonder.

Michelle Jobson (15)
Arthur Terry School

Gone Forever!

Gone forever are the days when you'd choose,
To sit and watch your child changing their shoes,
When you could walk out the house,
To think on your own,
But now you must never wander alone.

Gone are the times, when you'd walk down the street,
Rubbish in the bins, not at your feet,
Feeling so lucky, safe on your own,
Frightened of nullity, on your way home.

But times have altered, no more times on your own,
'Stay safe,' says the copper, 'don't walk home alone.'
'Be back by nine,' says your mom and your dad.
'Stay out of trouble and don't you be bad,'
You feel like a toddler, being watched all the time.
'Don't worry,' you say, 'I'll be back by half nine.'

Anna-Marie Ramsey (14)
Arthur Terry School

Gone Forever

Looking back at photos
I cringe as I think . . .
What was I wearing?

But I didn't care then.

Then was a time when
Naïveté and innocence
Protected us

From modern-day offence

Then was a time when
What you looked like
Was never a matter

There was a confidence that no one could shatter

Then was a time when
A make-up free face was cool
And comfortable clothes

Were the most fashionable to you.

Now is a time where
TV and magazines
Beautiful models and actresses
(Ones you look like in your dreams)

With their glittering glamour
And perfect frames
Poison the minds of young girls,
Infecting their brains.

And make them believe that they,
As themselves,
Are not good enough
To face the world.

Looking back at photos
I cringe . . .
But I wish I was still
That little girl.

Jennifer Williams (15)
Arthur Terry School

Gone Forever

When I was a girl I used to play in the street,
For hours and hours on end,
I would play out till late,
Mum knew I was safe,
Many a night I would spend.

I would play in the park,
Or in the dark woods,
Or even outside my house,
Not a thing troubled me,
I really felt free,
Those years were the best of my life.

Now I am older and have kids of my own,
But they are not allowed out like me.
No way are they safe to stay out till late,
Not with all the weirdos roaming free.

For if I let go,
To play in the street,
I doubt I will ever endeavour.
For if things went wrong,
The nights will be long
And my babies will be gone forever.

Katie Vaughan (16)
Arthur Terry School

Gone Forever

As I once stood upon that very hill,
Looking into a wonderful view,
Seeing all those beautiful trees and animals.

Now all I see is buildings,
No more trees,
No more animals,
Buildings,
Buildings!

It was such a grand view,
Now it just looks so ordinary,
All you see is lots of houses,
Once where an elegant forest was,
You once could see the birds on the top of the trees,
Now there is a local supermarket where those trees were,
Where there was a small winding river,
Stands a building which sells books,
You used to see many people upon this hill,
Now you hardly ever see anyone,
That wonderful view has now
Gone forever,
Gone forever.

Dan Hall (15)
Arthur Terry School

Pause In Time

Running around, no time to wait,
Second to second and never late,
Light now slow, or is it just you
Unable to breathe as there's so much to do?
          Pause in time, a blink of an eye,
          Just take a moment, to look at the sky.

24/7 all you do is run,
You can't stop until you're done,
You no longer talk to those you love
When will you have time? When you're up above?
          Pause in time, a blink of an eye,
          Just take a moment, to look at the sky.

Crashing sounds that never end,
E-mails not written yet ready to send,
A world always buzzing yet eternally asleep
With noise piled high, miles deep,
          Pause in time, a blink of an eye,
          Just take a moment, to look at the sky.

Danielle Howes (15)
Arthur Terry School

On The Beach!

I closed my eyes
And listened to the gentle waves move,
Swish, swash, the water moved,
The sun was beaming down on the bright blue sea,
The birds were singing, and the crabs were minging,
The sand was hot and ever so soft,
The sky was blue and oh so true,
As I open my eyes I'm lying there on the sand,
All I want is for you to take my hand,
The waves wash over my toes,
Washing away the pain,
I can hear the sound of the waves singing your name,
Now there's no one here to kiss you goodnight.

Lindsey Hill (14)
Arthur Terry School

Gone Forever

Remember those days when we played outside?
I'm standing here now those days have died!
Sound of cars
Darkened corners
Frantic mothers worrying inside
Are their children safe?
Where are they?
What are they doing?
The safety is going for children to walk the streets.

We're worrying and panicking for who they might meet.
Peering out windows into the darkness of the streets,
My heart starts to pick up the beats,
Everything is going . . .
The clock struck twelve,
Everything is going . . .
Slowly away
Sorry my child you cannot play
Everything has gone.

Gone forever!

Ashleigh Goldspink (15)
Arthur Terry School

Dragon

Ferocious and deadly,
Mighty and powerful,
Creating whirlwinds as it takes flight,
An enormous engine of destruction,
Swift and without mercy,
It slays its prey with one mighty slice,
Invincible, its skin unpenetrable,
Teeth as sharp as razor-sharp knives,
The ruler, of the sky.

Tumbi Okunribido (11)
Arthur Terry School

Gone Forever

Do the children of tomorrow play on the streets?

Gone forever are the joyous days of innocent youth as darkness
now stalks even the brightest of places

Do families still gather to eat and converse of what has happened
and what is to come?

Gone forever is the seemingly endless bond between kin as the day's
monotony wore slowly away like bacteria eating away at spoiled food

Does the beginning of the day henceforth bring clear beautiful skies?

Gone forever is the blue veil that once enveloped the sky now only
clouds of darkness are present to decorate the sky above

So what hath become of the world today, where children cannot laugh
and play, the land no longer basks beneath the sun and where the day
is a hard course to be run?

Well of the world that is now today it would seem what you once knew
is far away, the ways of the present seem heretical to the past, but
we all know good things don't last, so do we think of the good that
has gone or do we see it as what has begun?

Gone forever are the seeds of the past, it is our own folly that
we progress too fast.

John Duddy (15)
Arthur Terry School

Gone Forever

I remember when you could walk down the street,
No one there shouting abuse at your feet.
No one making fun of the clothes you wear,
Or the colour, length, style of your hair.

I remember when you could stand up in class
And people wouldn't make fun if you got a pass.
The rest of the class would clap and cheer,
Rather than the thought of passing becoming a fear.

I remember when a teen could go out at night,
Without being afraid of becoming the centre of a fight.
Children didn't use the bus stops and cider for fun,
Smoking, drinking and from the police they wouldn't run.

I remember when chat rooms used to be new,
Friendly and fun,
When old men pretending to be young boys
Was never ever done.
Children would do homework on the computer and
Hand it in on time,
Now they play on games and don't start work till half-past nine.

I remember when kids would use art for good,
Instead of using graffiti to tag on fences made of wood,
Kids wouldn't smash windows on people's houses
                              they didn't know
And round to their houses at Christmas singing
                         carols they would go.

I remember when children thought more of the
                              world around,
But now it's gone forever and children are
                    no longer safe and sound.

Becky Moran (15)
Arthur Terry School

Oh, What A World

Back in the day . . .

Back in the day, kids were out with no fear.
Now, they run scared from the man with his beer!
Oh, what a world!

Back in the day, Sunday afternoon at the bandstand.
Now, it's a mush pit on drug ridden ground.
Oh, what a world!

Back in the day, the radio would slightly crackle.
Now, it's dot com this and dial up hassle.
Oh, what a world.

Back in the day, for a sixpence an hour.
Now it's minimum wage and even less power.
Oh, what a world.

Back in the day, our country was strong
Now, it's 'Send them back to where they belong!'
Oh, what a world.

Oh what a world.

Jonathan Jacob (15)
Arthur Terry School

When The Kids Are Away
The Crisp Packets Will Play

When the kids are away the crisp packets will play,
They dance along the playground floor
Alive now and ever more,
The chocolate wrappers and apple cores,
Come out from their state of pause,
They hop around all day long,
Until they hear the children's song,
When they hear their merry little voices,
They go back to their fantastic poises.

Sheri Matthews (11)
Arthur Terry School

Gone Forever

No longer can they walk the streets,
                    Children on their own
For fear of a kidnapping or absence from the home.

Mobile phones for safety and if we need to call
But wouldn't you feel safer, if we didn't need those at all?

The closeness of a community, friends and neighbours alike
But never to share laughter again, just fight.

The countryside has gone, town and cities instead
One could maybe walk through allies of the dead.

The safety net to pick you up was made of love
Now just suffocation from the parent's harsh glove.

Where are the old days? We want them back
Fashion didn't matter, equality was a fact.

No longer can they walk the streets, children on their own
For fear of a kidnapping or absence from the home

Gone, gone forever.

Hannah Mackenzie-Grieve (15)
Arthur Terry School

Aeroplane!

Slowly wAlking through the airport
Arms and legs feel like jElly
I am dRagging and scraping my feet along
Anxious about taking Off
Tummy churning as I enter the Plane
Sitting on the plane, fasten your beLts
Three, two, one And lift-off
My throat is dry, I am in paiN
I feel like I can Explode
And they start to get more relaxed!
Slowly - slowly - slowly!

Sophie-Louise Purkiss (11)
Arthur Terry School

Not Your Problem!

People are dying and bombs are crashing,
But that's so far away,
Don't worry you say, the government helps
And you're subscribed to *Action Aid*.

I'd like to take you to that place,
That's just overseas,
Where children have machine guns
And mothers can't show their faces.

The desert there sticks red with blood,
Will it ever go away?
Tread wisely, friend be careful,
There are landmines where small children play.

Maybe then amongst the blood and guts,
You will realise,
What's as real as the life you live,
Does not have to be before your eyes.

Matt Orton (16)
Arthur Terry School

War

War is a terrible thing
There's no time to laugh and sing.

War is a nasty scene
It corrupts the daily routine.

War leaves people homeless and poor,
The enemy doesn't even know the score.

War leaves you with a bitter taste
It even creates a lot of waste.

War, there is no success
As a result there is only mess.

Chaos, destruction, even corruption.
Do you know why?

Matt Hughes (14)
Arthur Terry School

Gone Forever

Lost
The lone walk
Without being under the eye of the sick
The green of the land
Without the fog of pollution
The challenge of a task
Without the help of a false mind
The purity of a full line
Without short text entwined
The world
Without two sides in conflict
The freedom of life
Without being held back
Where have they all gone?
They've left now
Gone forever.

Kevin McDonald (15)
Arthur Terry School

A Kiss From A Rose

A kiss from a rose
Is so gentle and soft.

My feelings fly out
By that one kiss.

It tastes like strawberries
So sweet and nice.

It smells like roses
Drifting through me every night.

The red is so bright,
It makes my eyes water.

Every night I get a
Kiss from that rose.

Sallyanne West (11)
Arthur Terry School

What Is War?

What is war?
War is hate and anger,
The sound of aeroplanes dropping things over your head
Everyone is silent, listening and hoping
Then they are screaming out for help, for anyone
But no one comes,
All that is heard is a crash
Then there is silence again.

What is war?
War is guns and fighting
The sound of shouting and yelling
The shouting gets louder and the yelling more fierce,
They are coming, go quick,
We hear them getting closer,
But they are not quick enough
And gunshots are heard.

Victoria Everett (14)
Arthur Terry School

School Weekends

The school weekends are great
I'm going to go swimming
Teachers are at school marking all the books
Wishing the children wouldn't come back
All the children having fun
Five days a week
That's too long
I don't want to go back
I can't wait till half term
Just two weeks to go.

Yes!

Sarah Johnson (12)
Arthur Terry School

War

I could walk down the street on my own without watching my back,
I could wake up and not worry about what has happened to my family,
Friends and my village in the night,
I could look out of my window and not see any violence
Going on around me
I could walk around the village and see people looking
Healthy and no injuries.

The feeling of being able to play on the streets with my friends,
The feeling of wondering what's going to happen at school,
When I think about what I am going to have for breakfast in
The morning when I am lying in bed,
The choice of food that we can have and when we can have it,
I could go to sleep not thinking that I will never wake up.

Now I cannot walk down the street on my own and I always have to be
Watching my back getting ready for what's round the corner,
I now worry when I go to bed, thinking when I say goodnight to my
Family, is it the last thing I will say to them?
I am now too scared to look out of my window because of all the
Violence, I don't have a window, it has been demolished.

I am too scared to look at people when I am walking down the street
Because of their injuries and what they look like,
My family won't let me out into the streets with my friends because of
All the violence and they're scared in case I get hurt,
I don't get the feeling of my next school day because I don't have a
School to go to,
I don't get the choice of what I eat, our crops have been demolished
And our animals have died.
I wish all the fighting and violence would stop so me and my family can
Get back to normal but our lives have changed and war has caused
Permanent damage to our lives.

Lucy Smith (14)
Arthur Terry School

Two Different Worlds

Every thing is dry,
There's no water or food,
The crops are dead,
People are starving and thirsty,
They're hot, dusty and uncomfortable,
They'd do anything for a long, cold drink, a bath and water to wash in.

It's a rainy day,
Everybody's complaining that they're cold,
The crops are green and growing bigger,
The people go home to warm houses,
Where they can have a drink and a warm bath,
But they still complain.

They don't have to think about a drink, a bath,
Somewhere to wash or something to eat.

It's two different worlds.

Sophie Peters (14)
Arthur Terry School

The Local Derby

At the local derby there is always trouble,
But the atmosphere is electric.

My dad bought me a roasting hot cup of tea
And two sugars to make it dead milky.

We were into the game, my dad looked over,
I was shivering cold, my dad gave me his jacket.

I looked at him, he was in his shirt and he was cold,
But as long as I was warm it didn't matter.

It was a local derby I would never forget,
Me and my dad had the best time of our lives.

Josh Sherrington (11)
Arthur Terry School

The Changing Seasons

In the summertime
The sun starts to shine
The birds and the bees
Swarm out of the trees
Each boy and each girl shouts out with joy,
In the summertime.

In the springtime
The weather is fine
And all the flowers look divine
The mowers are busy cutting the lawn
In the springtime.

In the autumn time
Leaves fall off the trees
Many, many colours,
Float in the breeze
Days get longer
The wind gets stronger
In the autumn time.

In the wintertime
The snow starts to fall
And you all have to start wrapping up warm,
The days are getting shorter,
The nights are drawing in
And Christmas is near
So let's begin to celebrate the new year in,
In the wintertime.

Lauren Bayliss (14)
Arthur Terry School

Embarrassed

It's cold outside
And it's time for school,
I walk out the house
And I see a mouse,
To make matters worse,
I walk into a tree,
Not knowing that people are watching me,
I try and laugh it off,
But it doesn't work,
So I run back in the house
And lock the door,
I calm down for a bit
And look out the window,
See that they're not there,
So I go out for fresh air,
I hear giggles from behind,
So I turn around,
It's some girls from my class,
So I do a quick dash.

Laura Beddows (15)
Arthur Terry School

Journey Across The Desert
Escaping From My Life

Imagine:
You are walking forever under the hot, steamy sun,
Your mouth is dry and your head is burning,
Attacked by snakes and other lizards, this is no fun,
But imagine the thought of seeing more and maybe even learning.

You may wonder why,
I'm walking till I die,

But now you will see,
The reason was not me,

My life was a wreck,
As ugly as Shrek,

Because of the bullies I saw,
Big and hard and breaking some laws,

They had an attitude of a lion snarly and bad,
It wasn't long before I went mad,

Back then their hearts were made out of stone,
Their hearts must have weighed a tonne of horrid rock,
Remember bullies travel in flocks,

I was small and weak and felt so alone,
Those bullies were hard, right to the bone,

They:
Tormented,
Teased,
Kicked,
Threw,
Picked me up by neck,
Took the mick
And were generally being jerks.
So I packed my bags and left 'em alone,
Didn't even bother to give 'em a moan,

Now back to my trek,
The burning pain was beginning to rot my neck,

When I left, I left protected,
With 3 mutts and a knife,
Because my world isn't perfected,
It doesn't mean I've had a bad life.

Alex Etchells (14)
Arthur Terry School

What Were You Like As A Child?

Did you cry when you were born?
Were you tall or were you small?
When did you learn to laugh and talk?
When did you learn to stand and walk?
When you grow up what will you be?
Will you ever be able to say 'My family's proud of me?'

When I came into this world I didn't make a sound,
I didn't cry, there wasn't a tear in my eye,
Not like my brother who was born thin and tall,
I was born chubby, pink and small,
My dad said I smiled and laughed since the day
I was born, but I didn't start talking till I was one.
My first Christmas Day when I stood up as
I reached to get my plastic cup,
Then 3 months later I started to walk.
When I grow up I will be a hairdresser and beautician
That's a dream that could be,
I'm happy to say my family's proud of me!

Jodie Varley (14)
Arthur Terry School

War!

War, war,
It's so rough,
Land of courage,
Oh so tough,
Shattered, a daily routine,
People's minds will not be clean,
Fear of bombs dropping on your head,
Missed loved ones, are they being fed?
Helpless in every possible way,
Homeless, what can we say?
Trust in everyone
And we will get the day done.

Land of culture, poverty and sadness,
Hope the best of having gladness,
No people, quiet land,
No water or food in any hand,
Dried up their minds, put to rest,
Vietnam not at its best,
War, war,
It's so rough,
Land of courage,
Oh so tough.

Rebecca Humphreys (14)
Arthur Terry School

Paradise Beach

Warm, clear tropical waters,
Me, my mum and her friend's four daughters,
Sitting on a beach,
Right out of reach,
In the scorching hot sun,
Eating a sticky bun,
Luxurious yachts and a beautiful speed boat,
Right where the jellyfish float,
Smooth white sand,
Running through my hand,
The smell of coconut sun lotion
And tiny waves crashing down in a timed motion,
The tall palm trees swaying in the breeze,
Sorry, what a tease,
Clear blue sky,
Just you and I,
With the tropical fish,
That are a dreamy wish,
A coral reef,
With a sealife kingdom beneath,
I'm sitting right out of reach,
On a beautiful paradise beach!

Vicky Clifford (14)
Arthur Terry School

The Creature

The ground was still, it did not move anymore since it happened,
There was no sound now this had happened.
The noise you could have heard from miles away but now nothing.
The footprints that were like holes in the ground are now no more.
The trees don't get knocked down anymore.
Because of the men that came in their jeeps and trucks that day.
With their guns and nets to take these creatures down for good.
They went away and never came back, now they have
                                    what they came for.
The creatures just lie on the floor dead, with one
                        thing missing, their tusks.
The men even shot the ones that didn't have tusks
                        and what for? *Money.*
Now these creatures do not exist anymore now men have come.

Robert Tipping (14)
Arthur Terry School

Danger In The Sea

The sea is full of lapping waves,
Dredging sand and shells to the shore,
But what hurts me so is dolphins crying,
Seals dying,
All because of pollution.
The ocean is now a horrible black instead of a beautiful blue
And now instead of sand and shells
It's dead fish all around.
'Today's news,
An oil spillage happened this afternoon,'
That's what I heard today,
'150,000 fish and 200 dolphins *dead.'*
I wish I could do something,
Somehow, some way.

Jessica Faulkner (11)
Arthur Terry School

Sky View

Whizzing, whirling, zooming, hurling,
The bird flaps its wings as it sweetly sings,
The clouds take shape, they *morph*,
There's everything from cats to dogs.

Rubber meets tar, steel meets wind going at hurricane speed,
Noises rising, rising, fading, fading, fading,
Trees look like brown people with little green wigs,
What is that?

Bouncing, burling, booming, buzzing,
Such noises make my ears pop!
Oh clouds come down and make yourselves some earmuffs,
Rid these noises from my mind.

Crash! Creech! Clatter! Crush!
The noises of the road,
It would be much quieter up there in the sky,
Lucky birds.

I see a cloud like a cat,
I see a cloud like a rat,
How many clouds are there in the sky?
It would take a long time to count them all.

The noise of the ground,
The silence of the sky,
So much difference,
Are you both on Earth?

So much sound fills this minute planet,
What luck to be deaf,
No screams,
No disgusting slobbery noises.
But what about laughs,
Joyful sounds?

Stephanie Marie Malin (11)
Arthur Terry School

A Long Way To Go

She stumbled to the starting blocks,
The water looked deep and murky.

The gun went bang,
They all plunged into the water.

The other swimmers looked miles ahead
As they flew through the water.

A shower sprayed in her face,
As the person in front kicked her duck-like feet.

Her head turned as she looked behind her,
The starting block seemed so close but the end a long way to go.

She suddenly felt like a bird gliding along the deep water,
She darted round the corner and saw the finishing line.

On either side of the finishing line she could see the crowd,
They looked like a pack of meat-eating wolves.

The crowd's eyes looked like golden lanterns,
As they beamed at the swimmers.

Before she knew it, the finishing line was lifted above her head.
She'd won.

The crowd suddenly looked less fierce,
A gold shining medal was put over her head.

A long way to go was now finished.

Hannah Crowther (11)
Arthur Terry School

Oi!

Hi! My name is Oi!
Everyone tells me my name is Lucy,
But what do they know?
Nearly everyone calls me Oi!
My parents, some friends
And the kids who torment me
Shout at me, pick on me,
They say 'Oi! You, get over here,'
Then they kick me, punch me,
Steal my money, make me feel
Like the dirt on the floor,
Low and worthless.
I get angry, I see red, then they laugh,
I feel like there are insects
Inside me, squelching around
In my stomach.
I hate my tormentors, they make me sick,
I want to do to them what they do to me.
Kick them, punch them, steal their money.
So yes, my name is Oi!
Because I feel like Oi! inside.

Francesca Carnell (11)
Arthur Terry School

Winter

As the year ends and the sun falls
The cold winds creep up upon the trees
And whip their leaves down to the ground.

As the rain turns to hail
And the nights get colder
People have to wrap up warm,
So as not to freeze to death.

Then as the snow melts
The sun comes out again
And we are saved from the terror for another year.

Leanne Smewing (11)
Arthur Terry School

The Wind, The Rabbit And The Hunter!

Can you hear the wind today
Circling the leaves so they sway,
Left, right or back to front
Making it hard for hunters to hunt?
Bang, bang goes the hunter's gun,
He thinks there's a war but no one has won.
He's hunting for rabbits, birds or ducks,
He shoots down the burrows where nobody looks.
Run, run as fast as you can,
It's the big giant *man.*
Run, run, can't breathe, can't stop,
Can't be slow, can't go hop, hop.
I'm out of breath, I can't go on,
No one leave me all on my own,
That madman will shoot me.
He doesn't understand my rabbit squeak.
Will he take a peek?
I'm hiding in the bushes,
All he can hear is great loud mushes.

Sophie Ward (11)
Arthur Terry School

The Stormy Day

The window rustled, I looked outside,
The leaves were dancing and
swirling
round
and
round,
then up and down,
Dancing in the wind.
The bins were rumbling, they're coming to life,
Moving round.
It started to thunder, the light flashing,
Then died and I stood in silence.

Jenny Palmer (11)
Arthur Terry School

Winter Days

These winter nights are colder than ever,
The snow falls like a falling feather.
How I wish I could go outdoors
But every time I do down the snow pours
Like a thick sheet covering the land.
The snow is like little grains of sand,
My mum always tells me to wrap up good,
I don't like to wear them but I know I should.
Then it hit me, I'd make a snowman,
So suddenly into the house I ran,
Into the garage to get a shovel and pick,
Then into the kitchen where I would nick
A banana and an apple too.
As the night flew by I had to continue,
If I had to do it overnight I would,
I was going to do it as much as I could.
Then suddenly out of the blue, my mum called me in,
So I had to go and leave in sin.
I called to my mum downstairs, 'Goodnight.'
I went to sleep before switching off the light.

Matthew Perry (11)
Arthur Terry School

The Little Monster

There is a monster living in my house,
He likes to devour rubbish out of the bin,
He chews bones and munches stones,
He gobbles up rotten chicken.

He licks up milk as fast as a panther,
He licks dirty plates with his rotating, rasping tongue.
His fur is brown like gravy,
He makes me feel quite sick the way he swallows
His Chum and biscuits.

I love the little monster that lives in my house
Because that monster is my dog.

George Cutler (11)
Arthur Terry School

Who Am I?

Here I stand day after day,
Frightening all the birds away,
My hat is tall and very old,
Sometimes I get very cold.

Mice seem to think my straw legs are their home,
As in and out of my body they roam,
No cares have they for how I feel,
As long as they have warmth for their meal.

My coat is tatty and rather well worn,
As I stand amidst this field of corn,
The farmer chats to me now and again,
Whilst on my shoulder sits my friend - the wren.

I'm always here come rain or shine,
My withered hand has lost track of time,
The rustling trees let me know when a storm is coming,
As across the hills I see the rabbits running.

I am able to recount any weather story,
And can tell many a tale of triumphant glory,
What is my name - can't you guess?
Why *Scarecrow* of course - nothing less!

Matthew Eades (11)
Arthur Terry School

Your Soul Is Your Heart

Y our soul is your heart
O utside your heart is evil
U nholy is a word of evil
R ight in the centre.

S weet feelings become sweet words
O verjoyed is a feeling from the heart
U nselfish individuals are true lovers
L ove is a gift of life.

I nside your heart is the truth
S uspicion becomes confidence.

Y our soul is your heart
O utside your soul are false words
U nholy is a word of evil
R epulsive behaviour reveals the truth.

H e who gives his life
E motions come from inside
A ffectionate is a holy word
R ight in the centre are feelings
T ender, loving care.

Jade Tubb (11)
Arthur Terry School

Aliens

Aliens are here and there,
Some could be as big as a bear.
Some are black, some are green,
What colours have you seen?

In and out of ships,
They don't have any hips.
You've seen them in a book,
They could be on your hook.

They could be in your pipe,
So give it a good wipe.
Some might have hair,
Some might be *bare!*

Some might have fame,
Some might not have a name.
Aliens could be cool,
Some might have a special tool.

You might shiver
If they say they don't have a liver.
They could be a zoo keeper,
So bring in the Grim Reaper.

They might have a gun,
So kill him for fun.
They might have a funny head,
So stay tucked up in bed!

Sebastian Thornton (11)
Arthur Terry School

Lovely Flowers

Petals, as lovely
As could be!

Blue, pink, crimson,
Every colour you can think of!

Why? How can a
Flower be so beautiful?

The buzzy bees sinking into the rose
Like a person sinking into quicksand!

Why? How can a buttercup
Tell if you like butter or not?

The wonderful yellow sunflower,
Meadows like a yellow sheet.

I would like to be a flower in the park
To make people happy like me!

Philippa Ward (11)
Arthur Terry School

All Locked Up

I'm all locked up,
I can't get out,
I swallowed the key
And it won't come out.
People say I'm a sour grape
But I know that one day
My life will take shape.

Ellen Furley (11)
Arthur Terry School

Monkey Tricks Of No Mean Order

Deep in the jungle
Where the sun never shines
See the mighty monkey
Swinging on the vines.

Deep in the jungle
Climbing up the trees
See the mighty monkey
Bend her hairy knees.

Deep in the jungle
Where the tall tree grows
See the mighty monkey
Scratch her big fat nose.

Deep in the jungle
Hear the drums beat
See the mighty monkey
Shake her dancing feet.

Cherelle Leach (12)
Arthur Terry School

My First Day!

Whenever I wake up, every day before school,
I always dread the feeling of people calling me a fool,
I want to stay in bed every single dreading day,
It's not much fun being alone,
On the way to school I dread what people are going to say,
I see all the laughing people having a very happy day,
I get so mad that my skin turns cherry-red,
It's not much fun being alone,
Every day at lunchtime people always come up to me,
They hit and kick and always hurt me,
There is this vicious boy who is called tough Kenny,
It's not much fun being alone,
Kenny always tells me to give him all my lunch
Or he will give me a very hard punch,
I wish I knew why no one does really like me,
It's not much fun being alone.

Lee Turner (11)
Arthur Terry School

Lunchtime

It's lunchtime, what's on the menu today?
Scrumptious sandwiches of every kind,
Cracking cheeseburgers that will blow your mind!
French fries and pies, of which kind I can't decide,
Chicken or beef, it will be a feast.
Wonderful waffles with strawberry or chocolate sauce,
The choice is yours of course.
Just come and see what you can munch,
It is the best our school lunch!

Stephanie Evans (11)
Arthur Terry School

The Lynx And The Hunter

The lynx comes out from bushes,
His eyes like flickering lights.
He prowls through forest grass,
The tufts of ears are showing,
He goes to catch his prey,
But doesn't know of danger
That's entering the mountains.
The lynx climbs the tree,
He's ready to pounce on his prey.
Suddenly something comes nearer,
What could it be?
Man!

The man gets closer and closer and closer,
The lynx's heart pumps faster and faster,
The man's gun lifts higher and higher.
Boom! Boom! Boom! Pow!
He missed the lynx and shot the tree,
The lynx jumps out the tree and runs,
His long legs go as fast as they can,
The trees and bushes stopped the man.

He couldn't catch the lynx.
All that matters now
Is that the lynx lives,
Till man comes to invade
The lynx's home again . . .

Heather Lowe (11)
Arthur Terry School

Cheeky Monkeys

Cheeky monkeys
Dancing in the trees,
Swinging through the jungle
Chasing all the bees.

Causing mischief
Wherever they go,
Blow down the squirrel shelter,
One, two, blow!

Brown ones, black ones,
White ones too,
Millions of them everywhere,
Even in the zoo.

Scavengers, scoundrels,
They're not all bad,
Cute ones, happy ones,
Some are even sad.

Captured, behind bars,
They long to be free,
Wild and in the jungle
They all want to be!

Christopher Gerald (11)
Arthur Terry School

The Life Of A Ladybird

Whenever I am around
On or underground
Like jewels in the sunlight
And little beads in the night
Creeping, crawling around each day
On soil, leaves, wood and hay.

Whenever I am around
My friends the same
We're all the same red body, black spots
The way we know the way we go
Different ways, in and out
Different directions, out and about.

Whenever I am around
Green leaves, brown leaves, red leaves,
I am always there
In a dash, just like a hare.

Whenever I am around
The sound from underground
Rumbles through the ground and frightens all around
We scurry, we scamper, we dart here and there
We're frightened!

Hayley Humphries (11)
Arthur Terry School

Rainy Days

There's a leaf alone
Swinging from side to side
Up and down

There's a cat alone
Staring, walking up and down the road
Looking from side to side in the wind

There's a girl staring alone
Dreaming, moving in the wind
Side to side thinking

There's a miserable class
Thoughtless, listening to the wind
Staring at the rain in the puddles

Miserable winter days
Tip, tap, tip, tap
That's England today.

Mia Wright (11)
Arthur Terry School

The Firefly

The firefly passed through the dark night,
The sky was empty apart from the firefly's bright glow,
It was like a fairy light on a Christmas tree,
It flickered around and sped to a wall,
Where its future mate awaits.

Lucy Hipkiss (11)
Arthur Terry School

The Forest Spirit

The trees in the forest whispered,
The dying leaves flew through the air
A bush shook like something dived in
But no one at all was there.

As a squirrel I climbed the tall trees
Jumping from branch to branch
As a cumbersome hedgehog I crawled from my den
And carefully plodded along the floor.

Like thunder the men and machines came,
Trespassing into my land
Starting to cut down my children
And burning them to the ground.

With my beautiful world perished
I could clearly see
That my life was draining out of me
Goodbye, hope not to see you soon
I have a one-way ticket to a better place.

Paul Abbotts (12)
Bishop Vesey's Grammar School

Birmingham's Traffic

B irmingham
 I n the middle of the country
R ests this big, busy city
M y house is near the centre
 I n the middle of all the congestion
N o end to the cars, always one going by like ants on a hill
G od, how annoying, nowhere to play safely
H ow I long to move
A way from the congestion to a traffic-free area
M aybe, some day.

Adam Brownhill (12)
Bishop Vesey's Grammar School

Land Of The Dead

The red sun lay across the sky,
It knew that sunset now was nigh
And galloped off to places on high,
To await the dawn.

The sky was red
And in his bed,
Little Johnny rests his head,
As Mother entered the room he said,
'We're safe until the morning.'

Up, up, up it flew,
Through skies that were as black as pitch,
Unleashed a cry such as which,
Was heard never before or again.

The razor talons,
The hateful eyes,
Wreaked such havoc across the skies,
The fiery breath,
The stench of death,
That made it so despised.

Down, down, down it hurled,
To the tiny turquoise world,
Into Johnny's bedroom swift as light,
Then out again as dark as night.

The sky was black
And on his back,
Johnny lay upon a rack
And laid forever his little head,
For he was in the land of the dead.

Matthew Robinson (12)
Bishop Vesey's Grammar School

Best Christmas

The snow was crystal white.
The snow was falling with might.
The Christmas tree was glowing green.
This was the best Christmas I'd seen.

The cars had layers of ice.
The snow had turned to ice, which was nice.
There were children playing outside with solid ice.
One child got hit with ice, 'Ouch!' that wasn't nice.

The town was lit with bright lights.
Looking at the bright lights gave me bad eyesight.
The shops were closed which made a mighty fuss.
This was the best Christmas I'd seen.

I went to play outside.
My friends and I played rugby on ice, but I was offside.
My team scored five times.
The victory was mine.

This was the best Christmas I'd seen.

Nikesh Pokar (12)
Bishop Vesey's Grammar School

Drop-Book-Itus

Now here is something I just can't understand
When I pick up a book I put it straight back down
There is obviously something wrong with me
But what is it? I just can't see.
I thought a trip to the doctors would sort me out
But when I got there all he did was shout
He said I had a disease called drop-book-itus
So I went out and caught the bus
Straight back home to tell my mum
But she wasn't home, so it was just me
Lying on my bed wishing it hadn't happened to me.

Aaron Morris (12)
Bishop Vesey's Grammar School

The Way I Lived

It fluttered in the autumn wind,
The poor old thing was all alone
Standing there with no one
All its memories had been blown.

You would not notice it standing there
You would walk past it
As it watched in despair
It had no memories left.

One day the wind will take him
He will drift off silently into the night
Nobody will remember him
Nobody will care.

He will wake up one day and everything will be gone
Nothing there for him
Nothing there for them
Just the dew which falls from the tree.

He didn't want to go this way
It was the only way
There was a voice inside him which said, 'You can live a nice life.'
But I knew I couldn't.

I'd lived like this so I'll go like this
I'm just going to sit here
Let all the guilt and anger boil up inside me
There was only one way out, it was to stay here forever.

If only I'd been loved, I'd have never done this.

Tom Hurst (12)
Bishop Vesey's Grammar School

UFO Sighting!

UFO sightings,
Everywhere!
Strange disks floating
And flying through the air!

Turn on the news,
You'll hear all about it.
Mysterious disks spinning,
With flashing lights lit!

Maybe they're friendly,
Maybe not!
We need to prepare,
How much time have we got?

As I turned on the radio,
The reporter says, 'We're at war!'
And just at that moment,
Mom came busting through the door!

She said,
'Come on, come on, get into the car!
We need to go fast,
We need to drive far!'

'But why?' I asked
'Are we running away?'
She answered,
'Because, you idiot, they're landing *today*!'

So we drove and drove
And peered up at the sky,
But the crafts were leaving,
Without a single goodbye . . .

I wished they'd landed, we could have spoken,
'My name is Ogg, from the planet Zolon.'

Richard Kelly (12)
Bishop Vesey's Grammar School

Snow Surprise

The snow fell down and turned the grass from green to white!
The garden was looking nice and bright.
Children having fun, throwing snowballs,
On the dull and dark walls,
The snow was falling down like brown autumn leaves
Everyone was happy.

But how long was this going to stay?
Forever?
Or maybe never!
Who knows when the sun will come out?
Tomorrow?
Or today?
I peered at the sky
It was looking bright!
I thought to myself this is going to melt tonight!

As it went dark, the night closed its arms
Around us and the chilly air came in,
Everyone went to sleep peacefully,
Not knowing what surprise they would have
Tomorrow!

Habib-Ur-Rehman (12)
Bishop Vesey's Grammar School

The Countryside

The bright blue sky and green grass in the light,
rustling through the day.
The seeds of flowers growing,
with newborn sheep and cattle.

The horses standing, running fast,
with their hooves crashing down in the ground.
The freedom of what you want to do
and the way in which there is no one to moan.

How relaxing it is to draw, fish and watch the flowers bloom,
whilst you lie down in this warm air.
The colours of the flowers, red, yellow, orange, green and blue,
all the colours of the rainbow.

How lovely it is to be here
shame it's not for you!

Daniel Pryor (12)
Bishop Vesey's Grammar School

Grass

Grass is as green, as a glass of limeade,
Gleaming drops of dew, on each single blade.

The greener the grass, the more cows munch,
Chewing and chomping, as a salad for their lunch.

The lush green grass, likes to shimmer in the wind,
Like a wave of the sea, sweeping back out and in.

When winter comes, the lushness will die
And shrivelled brown patches will come creeping by.

These brown patches, as a monster in the shade,
Will then grow and grow, covering the whole glade.

The glade that was once green, grassy and warm,
Is now brown and dark, a dishevelled, dead lawn.

But when summer comes, back the green grass will creep,
Engulfing the brown grass, with a green salad for the sheep.

Alex Dalley (12)
Bishop Vesey's Grammar School

My Poem

What shall I write my poem about?
A town of Accra in a drought,
A poor old tramp starving to death
Or a very annoying girl named Beth.

It could be about an animal,
A lioness loving a strong male,
How about the deep blue ocean
Or even a fish in a swaying motion.

What about a grubby, old school
Or a bully who was certainly a fool,
The small, old rotten classrooms
Or my extremely messy bedroom!

It could be about my lovely home
With my interesting and small garden gnome.
Or my beautiful bright white bathroom
And then firework night with a *boom!*

How about a delicious Sunday roast
Or my big-headed brother who wants to boast.
An all day breakfast at the café
That is probably going to taste naff.

What can I write my poem about?
I could do nothing and write nowt!
There are so many things I could write,
It could be anything on the night.

Sam Griffiths (12)
Bishop Vesey's Grammar School

Guilty Conscience

It strays around the darkness,
Stalking in the night,
Evil as the fires in Hell,
Moves quickly as the night.

You will not know it's coming,
But you will know it's there,
Screeching in the shadows,
Vicious as a bear.

The wind will whisper hostile words
And put you into sorrow,
The guilt which lies upon your chest,
Will torture you tomorrow.

The walls and trees will speak to you,
Whenever you are near,
Their judgmental eyes that watch the world,
Will turn into a leer.

'So what is this great beast?' you ask,
'Which tortures all these lives
And makes the hairs upon your neck
Stick up like a thousand knives.'

It is your guilty conscience,
Of the dirty deeds you've done,
You try to keep it to yourself,
But your mind won't stay as one.

The moral of this story,
Which really is sublime,
Is do not do bad deeds,
For it is watching all the time.

Josh Storer (12)
Bishop Vesey's Grammar School

Pip's Pudden

Fear has an icy grip,
like no one wants to feel.
It hangs on to the stomach,
with a grip of steel.

Once a poor girl felt this feeling,
on a winter's day.
She was Pip, and was making pudding
for her mother, May.

The pudding had been apple pie,
with the best recipe.
But that young Pip, she couldn't cook
and filled it with honey.

When she saw her creation,
her body shook with panic.
The apple pie, freshly baked,
looked absolutely sick!

She knew the penalty for mistakes;
twenty days of chores.
She fled the house, scared as a mouse,
banging lots of doors.

Then she saw a Tesco shop
and cried with tears of joy.
She ran to the shop, bought a mop
and also bought a toy.

But also in her basket,
she carried an apple pie.
The packet opened, the good pie was cooked
and she had a nice long cry.

Andrew Marlow (12)
Bishop Vesey's Grammar School

The Great Fire

As I walked down my street,
I suddenly felt great heat.

Many fire engines rushed across,
I knew someone had a big loss.

The chain of fire engines was very long,
The rescuers in them were very strong.

These vehicles were in a great rush,
When they were gone there was a slight hush.

What was happening? I wanted to find out,
Suddenly I heard a great shout.

I wanted to explore what was happening,
My curiosity was widening.

I discovered that a house was on fire,
The people trapped were a lot higher.

The flames of the fire were so bright,
It looked like day in the middle of the night.

The trapped people the rescuers tried to save,
This showed that they were very brave.

'Help!' the people screamed,
Now the house was fully steamed.

The fire was out of control,
The house was very old.

A rescuer brought people down one by one,
One of them weighed 60 tonne.

As soon as the fire finished,
The whole house had vanished.

All the people were now safe and out of danger,
They thought that I was a complete stranger.

As the fire engines returned,
Towards my house I also turned.

Nabeel Nazir Ahmad (12)
Bishop Vesey's Grammar School

The Great Oak Tree

An oak stood in a field
its great green mane dancing in the wind
the brown arms never flinching
the Titan stood tall.

That night the blackness rumbled
the stars fled from the sky
in their place was lightning
coming with gifts of pandemonium and havoc.

Drum rolls echoed loudly
the lightning hit the buildings
slamming roofs to the floor
like German bombers had before.

Crack, bang, smash
an evil symphony
the thunder like a grenade exploding
the lightning a whip punishing the world.

This powerful attack was too much for the tree
the fat lady had sung
the lightning like a knife lunging at it
we heard a terrifying scream.

And early that morning I went to see
the mane scattered over the town
the arms were burnt to pieces
the grass was wet with blood
and the great oak was dead.

Ashley Bodenham (12)
Bishop Vesey's Grammar School

Food

The grass is green, the sky is blue,
I like food more than you.

Chocolate, chips, beans, it's your pick,
I could eat all day and never be sick.

Eat food, food, food all day
copy my eating habits and don't delay.

Sweets, biscuits and Coke,
empty the whole fridge along with cream cakes,
make sure that during the process
you don't eat a vegetable by mistake.

Slippery, slimy, slithering chocolate that glides down your throat
eat more and more and even more,
until you're eating like a goat.

Eat cakes, cakes and more cakes
that are as doughy as clay,
the chocolate cakes that I eat are like
mountains and a hot summer's day.

The grass is green, the sky is blue,
I know I like food more than you.

Aaron Dixon (12)
Bishop Vesey's Grammar School

School Holidays

After such a long term,
school is through;
so here I am on Monday morning
with nothing to do.

I lay back in my bed,
trying to sleep;
but I was woken when a car horn
went *beep, beep.*

I looked out my window to see
who honked their horn;
it was only my neighbours
pulling up right by their lawn.

I got up to brush my teeth
because my breath began to stink,
then I heard my door knocker
go *clank, clink.*

It was one of my friends
asking will I come out;
I had to have a shower
so I told him, 'Hang about.'

I went outside and met up
with all my mates,
that night I came home
a bit too late.

I like the holidays,
because there is no school
and I don't have to worry
about a single rule.

Amjad Khan (12)
Bishop Vesey's Grammar School

The Deserted Group

We don't know where we are
We don't know if home is near or far
Where shall we go?
Oh no! Oh no!

Someone is coming
We better start running
We could smell its breath
The droning smell of death.

We jumped in a boat
And put on our coats
We saw a big wave
We'd better be brave.

The wave has gone
We'd better be gone
We looked back
But there was only a sack.

Calum Macdonald (12)
Bishop Vesey's Grammar School

If I Could Have Five Wishes

If I could have five wishes
I know what they would be
I'd be a star and have a fancy car
And then there's number three.

I'd wish that I could have more cash
As much as Mr Abromovitch
And for my fourth, I'd wish to fly
Finally, there's my fifth wish.

I would ask to be fluent in French
In Latin and in German
The reason that I'd wish that wish;
Is so I wouldn't have to do the lessons!

Everyone's wishes are different
I'm just telling you mine
My dad, for example, would wish for some booze,
Whereas my mum would just wish for wine!

Matthew Coulthard (13)
Bishop Vesey's Grammar School

Life

As the rain falls down I'm huddled in my bed
Thoughts seem to rush aimlessly through my head.
My family have gone now, gone to a better place.
I can still picture them now locked in their final embrace.

So much deceit and so many lies.
I just wish sometimes, that I could be a bird in the skies.
I've lost my mom, my dad and my brother too
Why did it happen to me and not to you?

Life is a whirlwind, a hurricane, a storm.
There's times when you're happy and times when you're forlorn.
Sometimes it all seems pointless to me
But someone controls life and what will be will be.

Jack Ryan (12)
Bishop Vesey's Grammar School

The Forbidden Woods

In those forbidden woods where nobody goes,
There are evil things like goblins and trolls,
Werewolves and gremlins and black bats too,
It will give you a scare when the owl goes twit-twoo.

The tall, gnarled trees will tower like giants,
Blocking out the light of the moon so defiant.
A thousand tiny eyes glaring like jewels,
Nobody goes there - well only fools.

If the rustling and screeching doesn't give you a scare,
Then of the scraping and scratching you should beware,
A rearing up centaur, neighing in vain,
A small, tiny mouse squeaking in pain.

Don't stay here for long, here comes a troll,
Grunting and smashing with its long, spiky pole
A bony green goblin, smug and cunning
A grey little bird, hopping and running.

By morning it's returned to its eerie green glow,
No gremlins or goblins, werewolves? No!
Only the old gnarled trees remain in place
Come, play in the woods, now it is safe.

Sam Lumley (12)
Bishop Vesey's Grammar School

Fright In The Night

At night,
In the silent sky,
Are things which may give you a fright,
As you look out into the midnight light.

It could be a sparkling star,
Which always seems so far,
As you look out at them at night,
They twinkle and sparkle and seem so small,
Then you could maybe see one fall.

Then there's the moon,
Which looks like a big white balloon,
With its craters looking like cheese
And its glittery shine,
Which I find so fine.

Then there's the darkness all on its own,
It makes me feel like I am all alone,
As you look out at the black sky,
Its colour like a panther's black coat.

As you look out to the world tonight,
On a dark night like this,
There are many things that might give you a fright,
In the night.

Tom Jackson (12)
Bishop Vesey's Grammar School

Trees

A tree can be brown, green, yellow, red, orange or pink.
They stand so still and strong.
They have no minds
They can't do wrong.

If people were trees the world would be safer,
There would be no wars and no poverty,
All the world would be happy without sadness,
Which we know is caused by seething madness.

Trees know not about our cruel, complicated world,
Trees know only of reproduction and photosynthesis.
Trees may have their own language,
They communicate through each fallen leaf and each branch's swish.

If truth be told, we've ruined this world,
All the pathetic pollution and non-renewable resources is
                                        a pinless grenade.
If only we behaved more like trees,
Instead of always wanting what we see.

Trees are persistently perfect,
They stand by us but are we worth it?
Trees still stand tall and strong,
It is only that does the Earth wrong
For the bomb ticks on and on.

Simeon Wolfe (11)
Bishop Vesey's Grammar School

A Little Thing Called Love

There once was a boy in a whirl
He loved a very fine girl
He loved her so much
She wasn't very touched
Because all she wanted was to hurl.

Jack stalked her all day
His friends thought he was gay
So he bought her loads of stuff
She screamed, 'That's enough
Why can't you just go away?'

Jack was broken-hearted
All his mates did was farted
They didn't care at all
They just wanted to brawl
So he was back where he had started.

'No one understands
This girl, she's ruined my plans
I wanted romance
I wanted to dance
But now I'm all alone.'

In his pillow he would confide
About his beautiful bride
But then he realised his love
Was not actually a dove
She looked like a horse's behind.

Joshua Busst (13)
Bishop Vesey's Grammar School

Sleep Time

Sleep time, silence,
Not even a rustle,
Although in my head there's a hustle and a bustle,
My eyelids are heavy, but I'm wide awake,
Everything is going black,
Outside it certainly isn't day
And I'm drifting off, off . . . away.

Dragons, knights, saving princesses,
Elephants dancing in silly dresses,
Monsters, zombies, ghouls 'n' ghosts,
Me, a sea captain, sailing the coast,
Drunken mice running around,
Me, a pilot, landing to ground,
Two men in the west, duelling at noon,
Me, in space, walking on the moon,
Nibs, nobs, dib-dobs and things,
Me, in the clouds, halo and wings.

Sean Rhymes (11)
Bishop Walsh RC School

Red, Gold And Brown

Red is the colour of a rose
Red is the colour of a burning fire
Gold is the colour of butter
Gold is the colour of a diamond ring
Brown is the colour of a cup of tea
Brown is the colour of an old oak tree.

Joshua Smith (12)
Bishop Walsh RC School

The Good Days

Year 1: When I was one
I met David Dunn
Year 2: When I was two
I blew up the moon
Year 3: When I was three
I danced to the Black Eyed Peas.
Year 4: When I was four
My grandad was 50 and more.
Year 5: When I was five
I gave Elvis a high-five
Year 6: When I was six
Dad and Mom did some tricks
Year 7: When I was seven
George Best was 77.
Now I say goodbye
Because the rest makes me feel shy.

Rohan Farrell (11)
Bishop Walsh RC School

My Life

When I was one I weighed a tonne
When I was two I just started using the loo
When I was three I injured my knee
When I was four I trapped my finger in the door
When I was five I was glad to be alive
When I was six I played with sticks
When I was seven I thought about Heaven
When I was eight people called me Arron the Great
When I was nine I looked pretty fine
When I was ten I ate a fountain pen
When I was eleven it felt like I was seven
Now I am twelve . . .

Arron Mulready (12)
Bishop Walsh RC School

I Like Noise

I like noise
Noisy people in their big cars
Noisy pollution leaving scars
Noisy trains clicking on by
Noisy planes zooming through the sky
Noisy people at their home ground
Noisy people make too much sound
Noisy children riding their bikes
Noisy fishermen catching pikes
Noisy clocks tick-tocking on by
Noisy babies having a cry
Noisy animals in the zoo
Noisy people including *you!*
I like noise.

Christopher O'Day (11)
Bishop Walsh RC School

Noise

I hate noise,
The shouting of people,
The screeching of cars,
The moaning of children,
The screaming alarms,
The clatter of trains,
The crackle of fire,
The rustle of leaves,
The sound of a liar.

Christopher Brady (11)
Bishop Walsh RC School

When I Was Little . . .

When I was little,
I used to do
Anything I wanted to.

Make mud pies
Jump about
Tell big lies
Scream and shout . . .

Pull my hair
Hit my brother
Roar like bears
Annoy my mother . . .

Now I'm older and more mature
I cannot do these things anymore . . .

Sarah O'Connor (11)
Bishop Walsh RC School

Friends

They're there for you
They care for you
Have fun with you
When you feel blue
You all chill out
But may fall out
But friends are a precious thing!

Amy Dixon (11)
Bishop Walsh RC School

Hate

I hate monsters,
I hate going to bed,
I hate looking in my closet
I hate the scary dead.

I hate 8-legged spiders,
I hate my little sister,
I hate big bugs,
I hate my big, fat blister.

I hate going to school,
I hate the blues,
I hate being bored,
But I love the . . . Villa!

Hollie Patterson (12)
Bishop Walsh RC School

Childhood Memories

When I was *one* I had fun.
When I was *two* I could sit on the loo.
When I was *three* I ate a pea.
When I was *four* I fell on the floor.
When I was *five* I did a dive.
When I was *six* I picked up a stick.
When I was *seven* I ate a melon.
When I was *eight* I baked a cake.
When I was *nine* I looked fine.
When I was *ten* I got a new cat.
When I was *eleven* I looked for Heaven.

Cara Perry (11)
Bishop Walsh RC School

My Favourite Things

Swimming is my thing
I also love to sing
Running is the best
As I beat all the rest.

Aston Villa are cool
They will always rule
Blues are trashed
They always get thrashed.

I love Justin Timberlake
He always keeps me awake
I love to sing his songs
All day long.

That's enough of me
Let this be
A happy memory from me!

Erin Shakespeare (12)
Bishop Walsh RC School

My Nephew The Killer

My nephew Finn is a killer!
He really is a thriller!
He attacks me when I'm playing
And ow, he bites and spits at the same time!

He throws tantrums on the floor
And pins me up against the wall!
He opens doors just like our cat
We all call him Bo, just like Timbo!

He may be cute and podgy
But he really is quite dodgy
You have to watch out
And give out a shout
A one-year-old can be quite clever!

Shaheen O'Brien (11)
Bishop Walsh RC School

Childhood Seasons!

It's a new year,
What will the seasons bring?
The flowers,
The sun,
The leaves
And the snow bells that ring.

In spring I shall sing,
Sing to the flowers,
Climb up my garden tree
And ask my sister to play with me.

In summer I shall dance,
Dance in the midday sun,
Go in my paddling pool
And have some fun.

In autumn I shall read,
Read all day and read all night
And in the wind,
I'll fly my kite.

In winter I shall sleigh,
Down a hill in day, not night
And have some fun,
In a snowball fight.

It's a new year,
What will the seasons bring?
The flowers,
The sun,
The leaves
And the snow bells that ring.

Robert Walker (11)
Bishop Walsh RC School

Life

It seems the world grows uglier the wiser I grow
Or perhaps it's just where I'm situated and the people I know
There are millions of options, but which are right
If no human is perfect, then morally perhaps we have no sight?

How come science can fly a man into space?
But while they develop, they manage to destroy this place
As humans we're so ignorant, when the time comes blame is
                                        passed to another
But as long as ignorance is here, we will continue to 'discover'.

There is an old saying, which states, *you live and learn*
But perhaps there is no correct direction in which to turn
This is just one of the little questions playing on my mind
But unless the world changes dramatically then the answer
                                        I doubt I'll find.

The subject of this piece may not be entirely clear
But look a little deeper and your answer will soon appear!

Emma Anderson (17)
Bishop Walsh RC School

Childhood Memories

When I was small,
I hardly knew a thing at all,
But now I'm big and know everything,
To read hard books and spelling.

I sit at home and look back,
'Oh those good old childhood memories.'

James Cutajar (11)
Bishop Walsh RC School

The Heart Of England

Where the streets are paved with gold,
As the sound of a Birmingham tale is told:
The Bullring is open for all to see.
In you go for a shopping spree.
If it's another kind of ring you're after,
Take a trip to Hockleys jewellery quarter.
Celebrate a 100 years of Centenary Square.
Multicultural religions are everywhere.
Music is humming from Symphony Hall.
Where the proud BT Tower stands tall,
The smoke from industry away it's fled.
Canal barges rocking as bright as red.
Attractive suburbs with tree-lined streets,
Pretty gardens and comfortable seats.
Birmingham is the heart and shoots out like a dart,
But look how it competes,
It's better than the crowded ways of London streets.

Euphemia Carter (13)
Bishop Walsh RC School

Birmingham Poem

Birmingham has so much to give,
This is a place in which I am proud to live.
At the NEC and NIA,
The concerts or exhibitions guarantee a wonderful display.
Symphony Hall is famous for the sound,
That can be heard, all the way round.
Passionate fans support their teams,
At the rival football clubs, bursting at the seams.
If shopping is your favourite sport,
Look no further than the Bullring, Mailbox or the Fort.
You can travel to the city by car or train,
Or fly in from afar on an aeroplane.
Whatever you like, or wish to do,
Birmingham has something for you!

Natalie Durning (14)
Bishop Walsh RC School

I Like Bonfire Night

'I like Bonfire Night.'
The rockets scream,
The colours gleam,
The bonfire cracks,
The firework hitting the sky smacks.
A dozen fireworks clang,
A firework bursting, bangs,
A Catherine wheel whizzes,
A sparkler fizzes.
The sky is filled with light,
As people's faces are covered with fright,
The sky shimmers
And also glimmers.
'I like Bonfire Night.'

Faye Piper (11)
Bishop Walsh RC School

I Hate Noise

I hate noise.
I really hate the sound of pop
It brings my anger to the top.
The never-ending roar of rap,
Always sung by some young chap.
That dreadful racket of a juke box,
Or the deep mooing of an ox.
The loud noise of a machine gun,
Or the slow rising of the sun.
The shouting of a football chant,
Or my old grandma having a rant.
The hissing of a steam train,
Or the quick swish of a cane.
I hate noise.

Marcus Prince (11)
Bishop Walsh RC School

Christmas!

I like Christmas!
Walking through crunching snow,
Santa's shouting, 'Ho, ho, ho!'
People being pleasant,
Ripping open the presents!
Bells are ringing, *ring, ring, ring*
People starting to sing!
Sitting by the crackling fire,
People aren't ready to tire!
Come on everybody let's ski,
I see snow around me!
Hang your tinsel and your holly,
Everyone is jolly!
I like Christmas!

Hannah Griffiths (12)
Bishop Walsh RC School

I Hate Noise

I hate noise
The pop stars singing
The doorbell ringing
The referee's whistle
The blowing of a thistle
The sound of a stamp
The lock of a clamp
The baby's cry
The old man's sigh
The hissing of a lorry
The clanging of a trolley
The noises of today and tomorrow
Fill my heart with such sorrow
I hate noise.

Joshua Clayton (11)
Bishop Walsh RC School

Fireworks

I like noise
The shooting of a firework,
The pop of a wine cork,
The firework shooting into the sky,
The people down below look up high,
The bang in the sky and crackle,
The boys playing football, what a tackle,
The children holding sparklers in their hand,
The fireworks banging, looking so grand,
The dark night lit up by light,
The small animals hide in fright,
The night is quiet,
The people go home tired,
I like noise.

Natalie Milinkovic (11)
Bishop Walsh RC School

I Hate Noise

I hate noise
When people turn their stereos on at night
And in the morning you're not so bright
When lots of planes fly overhead,
It scares you so you're almost dead.
When the neighbours doors go *slam*,
You think it could bring down a dam.
When people shout across the road,
Or in the garden, there's an awful toad.
When you splodge straight through the mud,
Or when someone peels a spud.
Noise is awful, noise is bad,
When I hear noise, it makes me mad!
I hate noise.

Mitchell Thomas (11)
Bishop Walsh RC School

Why Is There Noise?

Why is there noise?
The rustle of leaves,
the clatter of keys,
so early in the morn,
but Mum still beeps her horn.
The speed of a lorry,
everyone's in a hurry,
I reach for the car door,
turn key, the engine roars!
The vibrant traffic lights,
schoolboys having fights,
radio volume blasts,
the school bus driving past.
The noise of a train,
blood rushing to my brain,
the squeak of the rubber tyres,
but from school, I'm still miles!
Why is there noise?

Catherine Teague (11)
Bishop Walsh RC School

I Hate Noise!

I hate noise!
Quiet people, they're too shy,
Noisy people make me cry,
Loud people who have a fight,
Loud people who shout at night,
Noisy people in the pub,
Toddlers chomping on their grub
Loud mobiles that all ring,
Chanting people in the crowd,
Noisy pets in the sports ground,
Noisy pets that bark and purr,
Chaos - children in the park,
I hate noise!

Joshua McKenna (11)
Bishop Walsh RC School

I Like Animals' Noise

I like noise,
The squeak of a mouse, the bark of a dog,
The roar of a lion, the croak of a frog.
I like it when the crow is crowing,
The song of a bird, like water is flowing.
And when the sun goes down and more animals appear,
That is when I listen harder to hear
The hoot of an owl looking for food,
The fox is rustling, the animals are scared.
For he might eat them, some aren't aware
Of his sharp, long teeth that cut and shred
It's scary out there, I'd prefer to be here in bed
Where I listen carefully to the noise of the night
And in the day the birds in flight . . .
I like noise.

Declan Whitaker (11)
Bishop Walsh RC School

I Like Noise

I like noise
The tortured screams of a man's soul,
The swoosh of axes and dropping of heads that roll.
The chugga, chugga of a big steam train,
The final shrieks of a man in pain.
The bang, bang, bang of a shooting commander,
The crunching and munching of a noisy panda.
The screeching of brakes, the crunching of metal,
The high-pitched whistling of a boiling kettle.
The wailing of winds, the rustling in the leaves,
The crying in agony of falling trees.
The clashing of bone, the splurting of sinew,
The crying and wailing of a sinking crew.
I like noise.

David Carey (11)
Bishop Walsh RC School

I Love Christmas Noise

I love Christmas noise
Christmas began when Jesus lay
Sleeping soundly on the hay.
Snow is falling all around,
Laid out smoothly on the ground.
Icy cold tingling frost,
Ring of the tills, expensive cost.
Presents hidden, time for the search
Soon all the family are gathering at church.
Santa's ho, hos as the sleighbells ring
Travelling door to door choir boys sing.
Crisp and ripe the dinner cooks
Children reading Christmas books
Toys are moving round and round,
Gifts are coming in leaps and bounds
Christmas trees are shedding their pines,
Xmas lights flickering on signs.
Greetings shared as we eat our dinner
At Christmas time everyone's a winner
Mistletoe kisses to say goodbye
Up the stairs with a moan and a sigh
Pull back the sheets, count the sheep
Tonight will be my soundest of sleeps.
Dreaming of this Christmas Day
That started when Jesus lay
Sleeping soundly on the hay
I love Christmas noise.

Laura Dale (11)
Bishop Walsh RC School

I Like Noise At The Beach

I like *noise!*
The cry of a baby, the cram of the crowd,
As people arrive, the volume gets loud,
The swaying of water, the crunch of the weed,
The shells on the seashore, as small as a bead.
The thud of the ball, hit the volleyball team,
As they end with a win and the fans all scream.
The good little girl, all alone on her seat,
Waits patiently for her parents while swinging her feet.
As crowds separate, the *noise* becomes low,
The last family walks home very slow.
Rubbish is left, who's to clean up the mess?
It's only one person's job, why don't you guess?
I like *noise!*

Kelly Collumb (12)
Bishop Walsh RC School

I Like Noise

I like noise
The show is ready to commence,
As the Catherine wheel goes round the fence,
As the sky gets dark on a cloudy night,
The little children are given a fright,
As people open their drinks that fizz,
The powerful rockets go up and then whizz,
As they go up fast and end up high,
The fireworks will bang loud from the sky,
As the grand finale opens up ad glimmers,
The audience's faces are left from the shimmers,
A clap comes from a group of boys,
As the girls hearts bang out of joys,
I like noise.

Jodie Prinsep (11)
Bishop Walsh RC School

The Flower

F lourishing in the summer air,
L oving the gardener's tender care,
O ver the grass they bend their stem,
W ith their buds peeping below them,
E mbarking on the cold, wet ground,
R ed and yellow petals to be found.

P etals prosper in the summer sun,
E very flower to have its fun,
T owering above the long green grass,
A s the small butterflies flutter past,
L asting in the summer glow,
S adly, fading away into the winter snow.

Sophie Patterson (12)
Bishop Walsh RC School

History

H is for historians, the brightest of the bunch,
I is for the Incas, who ate humans for lunch.
S is for sources, which help you in class,
T is for the Tudors, who argued over Mass.
O is for operations, which help you win a war,
R is for revolutions, when you overtake the law.
Y is for Yankees who made history in the west,
   All these are *history,* they make it the best.

James Dickenson (13)
Bishop Walsh RC School

Old Omaha

Old Omaha stands now against him,
In his wake, the Axis mines.
The sand of traps and wire,
And eliminating enemy lines.

The smell of burnt-out tanks,
The sound of souls in pain.
The taste of death is here with him -
Bodies fall and blood is as rain.

Memories of past shoot across,
With bullets and shells mixed in.
Operators fearing the worst at home,
Ready to call next of kin.

The jubilant Canadians at Gold,
The joyous British at Sword.
Old Omaha wasn't so lucky,
Six thousand to meet thy Lord.

Dan Howl (12)
Bishop Walsh RC School

My Car

My car is a lion roaring down the M6,
As it goes it is chewing on a Twix.

It screams round the corners at 200mph,
This car has lots of horse power.

The cops are on my tail,
Will I lose them or will I fail?

I accelerate down a long straight,
The cops are coming closer, scratching off the paint.

As my car gets totalled, I scream:
'This is only the PS2, but I can always dream!'

Andrew Dennis (12)
Bishop Walsh RC School

The Autumn Tree

It was a mild autumn day,
On the floor the leaves lay.

The leafless tree,
Stood there in all its glee.

The skeleton frame
Stood without shame.

The brown, crusty bark hides its historical years,
Its life be told all its hopes and fears.

The trunk was tall,
It had been battered in the fall.

The roots are there to keep it still,
So that it doesn't fall and kill.

The tree has fought in every way,
To live and thrive another day.

Jack Knight (13)
Bishop Walsh RC School

Tigrrr

Her sleek yet coarse agile frame
Hunting for her lunch again
Crouching, camouflaged, watching, waiting
She suddenly springs up with great ease
Her dinner awaits her within the trees.
She darts towards where her prey is sat
It tries to escape this strong, ravenous cat,
But the creature fights for life in vain.
The tiger is satisfied once again.

Emma Bagley (12)
Bishop Walsh RC School

A Normal Day At School

The light goes on
The alarm bell rings,
'Get out of bed,' my mother sings.

6.30am, still dark outside,
Snug and warm in my bed,
But for how long can I hide?

Curtains are drawn,
The street light shines in,
'Get up, get dressed!'
Time for the new day to begin.

Run for the bus
Just caught it in time.
Won't miss registration
I'll be there for nine.

First lesson begins, it's German today,
But I've done my homework,
So everything should be okay.

Next lesson was science, oh what a bore,
Seems like I learned everything before.

Fifteen minute break at last
But pretty soon that time had passed.

Drama was next, that was so much fun,
Then came lunch and out came the sun.

The next two lessons dragged on and on,
Can't wait for the bell when I'll be gone.

The end of the day came at last,
Now it was all in the past.

Back at home, have some tea,
Homework's done, watch TV.

Jenna Clewley (12)
Bishop Walsh RC School

A Seal's Short Life

I am a baby seal
Just dozing on the ice,
The trouble is with me
My fur is awfully nice.

I can hear footsteps
Not that far away,
I think it's those nasty men
Who took my dad away.

I used to have a dad,
Two sisters and a brother,
Oh dear, they're coming closer
I think they want my mother.

He's got a stake in his hand,
To put in my head,
My white coat will soon be blood-red.

Kelly Riddington (13)
Bishop Walsh RC School

Crying . . .

Your mouth dries up
You can only whimper.

As your face turns red
You can hear curious whispers.

Your eyes go blurry
You can barely see.

You hold your breath
As a tear rolls silently down a rosy face.

Jade Clark (12)
Bishop Walsh RC School

Amazing Space

Stars, stars oh so bright
Stars, stars, light up the night
Stars, stars, dazzle the air
Stars, stars, oh so rare.

Moon, moon moves through the sky
Moon, moon passing by
Moon, moon round as a ball
Moon, moon standing tall.

Earth, Earth green and blue
Earth, Earth, each day new
Earth, Earth, land sky and sea
Earth, Earth, you fascinate me.

Hannah Twist (12)
Bishop Walsh RC School

What Will Happen?

Sunday's the day, it will be bright,
But please, we hope, no one will fight.
We should all be friends,
We know we should
But really it's different.
We knew that it would
Take your lucky mascot and your flag,
Drinks, crisps and biscuits in your bag.
Get ready to cheer
And face the fear.
So what will happen and who will lose -
Will it be *Villa* or will it be *Blues*?

Elizabeth Woodall (12)
Bishop Walsh RC School

Untitled

Star City is brill
You can have a good thrill.

In the *Snowdome* you will crash
Off the wall

So make sure you don't fall.

Sports And Leisure is a pleasure
So get off your seat
And live forever.

At the *Villa*
You will see
How good we can be.

When *Villa* plays the *Blues*
It is like we're on a cruise.

The NEC is the place to be
With a happy family.

New Street Station
Is the heart of the nation
Taking people to their destination.

Go to the *Fort Shopping*
Has all the bargain hunters hopping
If you have time to spare.

Liam Gough (13)
Bishop Walsh RC School

Green, Red, Black

Green grass shining in a field,
Trees swinging in the wind.
Green, the colour of the Jolly
Green Giant.

Red cars speeding down the road,
The red sun, hot in the evening sky.
Red blood, freshly cut.

Black as the Devil's right hand,
Black cat, known as bad luck.
Black as the midnight sky.

Theo Caines (12)
Bishop Walsh RC School

Green

The green grass shines in the sun
Green is the colour of a shamrock
It is also the colour of a green apple
As green as Shrek's skin
A green leaf off a tree branch
A piece of green, crunchy lettuce
The colour green is like a grape
Green is the same colour as green paper.

Kerri Richards (12)
Bishop Walsh RC School

Dog

He has a pink nose,
He'd look funny wearing clothes
He has big brown eyes
Loves the taste of pies.

He has golden fur,
And sometimes purrs,
His name is Ben,
His best mate is Len.

Ben loves to play
In the field with Faye.
Then has a nap
And his ears flap.

Dinner, yum-yum
The taste is quite fun.
Smells really good,
Now for his pud.

Ben's out in the garden
He saw the cat named 'Fardom'
They had a good chase,
Now Ben's lost his good pace.

Laura Dudley (12)
Bishop Walsh RC School

I Hate Noise!

Why must we debate on noises I hate?
Like trains going clink-clack,
Or the noise of someone's back
and people groaning.
But the worst is my sister, moaning,
I hate noise!

Luke Moscrop (11)
Bishop Walsh RC School

I Like Noise

The rustle of the trees,
The crackle of the leaves.
The bibbing of a horn
Of a car at dawn.
A bike of screeching brakes
And an animal that shakes.
The cork that pops
The kangaroo that hops.
When the silence destroys,
The soul-stirring joys.
The thud of a hoof
On a galvanised roof.
I like noise.

Pierce Brennan (11)
Bishop Walsh RC School

Autumn

Autumn leaves fill the sky,
Reds, yellows, low and high.
Crunching leaves cover the floor,
Watch and walk all in awe.
Windy, sunny and autumn rain
Autumn fun hard to explain.

Joanna Maguire (12)
Bishop Walsh RC School

The Weekend!

Yes, at last I can have a lie in,
Just a few extra hours aren't a sin.
Everywhere is quiet, not counting the snoring!
This is what happens on a Saturday morning.

Then a lot later, I meet my friends,
The cinema, the shops, our fun never ends!
Then McDonald's for our lunch,
You'll never have met a hungrier bunch.

Then I go home to relax once more,
Watching TV is never a bore.
Whatever the programme,
In Heaven is where I always am!

Eventually Mom starts to moan,
'Your room's a mess, it makes me groan!'
Tidying up is such a chore,
Sweet wrappers, CDs, there's mess galore!

When at last you can see the carpet,
On my bed I go and sit.
Out of nowhere my stomach starts to rumble,
I go to Mom and start to grumble.

A fancy restaurant, we go to eat,
With high-heeled sandals on our feet.
The food tastes so good on an empty tum,
Oh my Saturday has been such fun!

Anna McDonagh (13)
Bishop Walsh RC School

Friends

Friends are special people who help you
when you're down,
They take you out, make you laugh, and
bring you into town.
Friends come in all different sizes, wherever
you will meet,
At school, in the park or even on the street.

Friends are like rare flowers that bloom on only
one high mountain,
Treasure it and it will shower you with rare
friendship, like a fountain.

To your friends be thoughtful, kind and true,
If you do this they will be just as nice to you!

Eloise Payak (13)
Bishop Walsh RC School

Autumn

A quilt of leaves covers the ground,
The wind whisks them up, they swirl round and round.
A crisp rustling sound they make,
They are gathered into piles, using a rake.

Red, yellow, orange, brown and gold,
In the blustery autumn cold.
They are blown to the ground without a sound,
A variety of fruits from trees, falls ripe,
Apples, pears and chestnuts, I like.

Alexandra Rowledge (12)
Bishop Walsh RC School

Sandstorm

Sand is blowing everywhere,
In the desert which is so bare,

Camels are closing their eyelids tight,
Against the sand and the blinding light.

There are winds of sand and heat,
Which you wish you could defeat.

As you're walking into the gust
It is pushing you back, like a thrust.

Sand is digging into your skin
And you just wish for a layer so thin.

Sand is a fearful thing,
And I advise you, it will sting!

James McCulloch (12)
Bishop Walsh RC School

The Teacher

Still no teacher, it's been half an hour,
Maybe he's ill or stuck in the shower.
Then a tall man strode through the door
Only to fall straight to the floor.
Standing up, his glasses askew,
He said, 'Excuse me, are you class two?'
He started to speak but got lost halfway,
It was evidently going to be a very long day!
He turned to the board, scribbled and wrote
He coughed and spluttered, 'I've a frog in my throat.'
We looked at each other and started to grin,
Soon this grew into an unbearable din.
'Stop talking boy! What's the matter with you?'
'Sorry sir, but well - we're not class two!'

Joe Martin (12)
Bishop Walsh RC School

The End

It closed on me before I knew it,
The darkness,
As the light faded away.
The silence,
As the voices drew away.

It closed on me before I knew it,
Compressing, suppressing;
Bearing down, heavily,
Thoughtless, uncaring,
Callously sneering.

It closed on me before I knew it,
My throat constricted,
From sheer terror.
I kicked and connected,
Only the walls of my narrow jail.

It closed on me before I knew it,
And dawned on me finally,
Creating dread as I realised;
From this cell at least,
There was no escape.

The beginning?

Fatima Shaikh (17)
Broadway School (Sixth Form)

The Lion And The Monkey

The lion said, 'Yo!'
The monkey said, 'No!'
The monkey fell out the tree

The lion said, 'Yum!'
The monkey was in his tum
It was too dark for the monkey to see

The monkey screamed for help
But no animals' ears felt
The poor monkey's desperate pleas

So the monkey bit a hole
This was the golden goal
The monkey escaped, injury free

The lion said, 'Hey?'
But the monkey had run away
And the lion felt very lonely.

Jaspreet Randhawa (15)
Codsall Community High School

No One's Butterfly

Flying here and flying there,
This beautiful butterfly is flying everywhere.
It is going somewhere but where he doesn't know.

It's colours are red, orange, brown and white,
When people walk past him they give him quite a fright.

He lands softly on a flower, like a leaf falling on the ground,
He is as quiet as a mouse, he makes no sound.
It is a wonderful sight to see him there,
He is all alone, fast asleep and no one seems to care.

This butterfly is alone every day and night,
He now dreams of meeting a friend . . . one day he just might.

Jenny Synnott (13)
Codsall Community High School

Black And White

Black and white
They're only colours,
Despite what many may say.

Black and white
Both have the same rights,
Despite what many may say.

Black and white
Aren't opposites like day and night,
Despite what many may say.

Black and white
Are just alike in more than one way,
Despite what many may say.

Black and white
Should be seen in exactly the same light,
Despite what many may say.

Black and white
Should never fight in any kind of way
Despite what many may say.

Black and white
Don't forget they're only colours,
Despite what many may say.

Monique Stewart (15)
Codsall Community High School

Panda

The rare and giant panda
It's like a teddy bear
But if you get too close
It may kill you, so beware!

Panda's are playful
Jumping through the trees
Playing with other pandas
Sleeping in the breeze

A panda's life is simple
They live their life with ease
The main three things they do
Are eat, sleep and breath

It sits among the trees
Eating the bamboo
Sitting there quietly
When along comes a poacher and shoots

They are used for fur
And for their meat
Because these cruel people
Have too much greed

A panda then is killed
Another one is shot
If it keeps on happening
The species will be gone!

James Yardley (14)
Codsall Commnity High School

Have You Ever?

Have you ever seen a dolphin
Cutting through the velvety sea?
Have you ever seen a dolphin
In Sea World, waiting for its tea?
Have you ever seen a dolphin?
Jumping high through the sweet sea air?
Have you ever seen a dolphin?
Look around, they're everywhere!

Have you ever touched a dolphin -
Ever touched their sweet, smiling face?
Have you ever touched a dolphin?
They're silky, like a dress of lace.
Have you ever touched a dolphin?
They're gentle, calm and take great care.
Have you ever touched a dolphin?
Look around, they're everywhere!

Hannah Rogers (14)
Codsall Community High School

The Clouds

Cotton wool dotted in the sky,
Some stay all day, others pass by,
Whether they're grey or whether they're white,
They fade into the sunset night.

Depending on the mood they take,
The sun may suddenly start to break,
If the Arctic winds should blow
The clouds may start to shed their snow.

Some clouds depict familiar faces,
Changing shape and changing places.
If I could float like a cloud above,
That is a wish I would love.

Laura Mathews (13)
Codsall Community High School

Cats

Black as night and as white as snow
Brilliant green eyes that glow in the dark

Cats!

They curl up in front of the fire like a ball of fluff

Cats!

Attack with claws when in fear of danger
Though rarely happens when in loving homes

Cats!

Spend almost all of the day sleeping
Take care of washing themselves

Cats

Loveable, kind, friendly, fussy, always around

Cats!

Anne Renton (13)
Codsall Community High School

I Love Little Pussy . . .

I love little pussy; her coat is so warm;
And if I don't hurt her, she'll do me no harm.

So I'll not pull her tail, nor drive her away
But pussy and I very gently will play.

She will sit by my side and I'll give her some food;
And she'll love me because I am gentle and good.

I'll pat pretty pussy and then she will purr;
And this shows her thanks for my kindness to her.

But I'll not pinch her ears, nor tread on her paw,
I will be gentle to her so she won't use her sharp claw.

I never will hurt her, nor make her displeased,
For pussy doesn't like to be worried and teased.

Ilona Hodson (14)
Codsall Community High School

Alone

All alone in the dark
Don't know who I am
What should I do?
Why don't I know who
They are?

They don't understand how I feel
They don't care what I think
How can I get out of this place?
I am neglected by all I know
Nobody cares where I've gone
But deep down inside I know who I am
And where I need to be

Trapped in this room
Where can I go? I need to be free
Can't see out at the world around
And I'll never be anyone at all
My appearance has changed since I came here
I seem pale, cold and aware
I've never felt like this before
I feel hatred for everyone, everything outside
I'll always be here for no one to see
Or share my life
Evermore!

Amie Farrington (13)
Codsall Community High School

Trapped

I am trapped in a room
and my best friend is a broom.
I'm on the edge
trimming a hedge
of my life.

I'm going out of my brain,
which is giving me pain.
I'm in deep sorrow,
I hope I see through tomorrow.

I don't eat
which is turning me into a thin piece of meat.
I don't drink
which makes me not want to wink.

Let me see
deep inside of me,
I hope I don't die
as these people pass me by.

As it goes into the night
it takes up all of my might,
to sleep
and of course weep.

When I think of food
it puts me in a bad mood,
me in my pyjamas
reminds me of bananas.

I can hear mice
they sound quite nice,
when I hear their feet
it makes me think of meat.

I am sitting here
I look out of the window and see a deer,
wondering if I will ever meet
my very good friend Pete.

Nick Francis (13)
Codsall Community High School

When I Look At Our World

When I look at our world,
What do I see?
Orphans with no mom or dad,
I think to myself, *what would that be like?*
It could be me -
Just think!

When I look at our world
What do I see?
New lives being born into this world
I think to myself, *what would this be like?*
The world multiplying, day by day
Just think!

When I look at our world,
What do I see?
Bullying and racism
I think to myself, *what would this be like?*
I wish everyone would get on with each other in our world,
Just think!

When I look at our world,
What do I see?
People dying and crying and living in poverty.
I think to myself, *what would this be like?*
People only wish for a normal life,
Just think!

When I look at our world,
What do I see?
I see love, happiness and care in our world,
I think to myself, *what would it be like?*
People together and friends forever,
Just think!

So when you look at our world,
Just think to yourself,
It's not the world itself that is an awful place,
There are some evil people in our world
Which make it a disgrace.
Just think!

Rebecca Owen (15)
Codsall Community High School

The World's Greatest Mystery

I often wonder when's the best time to go,
Young and eager and ready for anything?
Or old and tired and seen everything?
I often wonder what's the best way to go.
Heroically, suddenly and with a bang?
Or quiet, expectantly and without a fuss?

I don't know!

These questions really get me confused,
But it all depends on what awaits me afterwards.
Will I be taken to the light and wonderfully rewarded?
Or taken to the dark and brutally punished?
Will we all be taken to the same place?
Or will we be judged and parted from our friends?

I don't know!

Maybe there is no place to go,
Will we return to Earth in the form of another?
Perhaps even a dog, a fish, a tree.
What about ghosts? Will we return to haunt our heirs?
Or are they just another hoax?
But maybe after life that's it.
Finish, the end, cease!

I don't know!

It's the world's greatest mystery.

Michael Hobbs (13)
Codsall Community High School

Kidnapped

It was dark
It was cold
He was getting scared.

It was strange
It was hard
He was getting confused.

He was abused
He was neglected
He was getting angry.

He was in danger
He had been kidnapped
His name was Liam
Or was it Tug?
Or was it Phillip?

Who were these people?
Were they friends or foe?
Was it money or publicity
They wanted?

Was he here?
Was he there?
He could be anywhere.

Will he come home
Or will he die?
Or is he already dead?

Luke Greaves (14)
Codsall Community High School

Protecting The Foal

Galloping down the meadow,
With a breeze in his mane and tail,
He arrives at his herd and his white coat
Shimmers in the sun.
As he rears up playfully to greet the others,
His horsy whispers drift off into the distance,
He gathers them together as if protecting them from something.

His eyes widen
Nostrils flare
His ears flicker at the slightest noise.

Bang! Bang!

The herd gallop away, startled,
A foal drifts behind,
Struggling to keep up.

He sends a signal for his mum to lead,
He turns a sharp turn
He flees to the foal.

Bang! Bang!

The shots go off again
He leads the foal quickly towards the forest,
As he waits patiently guarding the foal, it goes quiet.

He raises his head with his ears pricked up like Pyramids.

He takes a step forward,
Twigs and leaves crackle beneath his hoof,
He starts to walk slowly,
Hesitating with every move.

The foal is right next to him
As if they were glued together
He leads the foal quickly into a cover of brambles
To protect him from any danger.

Jessica Thwaite (13)
Codsall Community High School

The Sea

The deep, dark green, blue underworld,
Has many different ways,
As it anxiously waits to attack,
In a subtle way, it moans and sways.

It's the sea's luxurious, profound ways,
That makes you wait and wait.
To hear many sounds of
Stormy, wavy and seagull sounds.

It's an intense, forceful place,
With a mysterious world.
Full secret of treasures,
And any new living creatures.

The way the waves dance so elegantly,
Sends you into a peaceful and tranquil glance.
Then in a quick, sudden flash
It sends you into a thrilling and powerful trance.

Three exhilarating waves hit the tall, tough, mighty cliffs,
With the sound of a shuddering clash,
Then it all departs and goes back to normal,
With all peace found at last.

Jessica Kataria (13)
Codsall Community High School

The Mind

The mind is an open door
A gateway to fun, joy and learning,
A controller of the body.
It can build, repair and destroy
A unique limitless organ.
It will take you round an obstacle
And remember it for next time.

A dreamer, risk taker, entertainer, improver,
But still fears its demise,
It will question its actions;
Think of people's reactions,
Make complex interactions,
To explore and to learn,
Way ahead of its time,
Brilliant and sublime,
But will fall into line,
To die as one or the other.

Joshua Priest (13)
Codsall Community High School

Too Young

She sits there, silently
Just watching 'Noddy'
She makes towers with her blocks
Then knocks them down and giggles.

I get her some juice
Then sit her down in her cot
When I leave the room
She screams, 'Alice!' and cries.

'Alice is at her friends.'
I try to tell her
But she doesn't understand
She's too young to know.

Charlie Ward (15)
Codsall Community High School

A Starry Night

As I looked out of my window
On a cold winter's night,
The sky was full of jewels,
It was the stars shining bright.

They were glistening and sparkling
In the cold, midnight air,
Some have got names
Like The Plough and The Bear.

The stars twinkled like candles,
With their wicks standing tall,
They all look different sizes,
Some large and some small.

I couldn't stop gazing
At this wonderful sight,
And wondering where the stars go
At the end of the night!

Emily Hadfield (13)
Codsall Community High School

Panther

P erched upon a boulder
A waiting his prey
N ever to know what's coming his way
T here people shouted
H ooting, jeering
E ager to catch their prey
R elief! It's dead.

Kellie Jones (13)
Codsall Community High School

Pony

Standing under an apple tree as still as a statue,
Suddenly the pony's ear flickers as a small sound is heard.
Without glancing behind, the pony gallops to the other side of the field,
The noise he makes is tremendous, but his hooves aren't always
                                        touching the ground.

He slows his pace down to a canter.
He is breathing heavily and his pure white coat is dripping with sweat.
He canters a few circles with his silver mane flaring in the wind
And his silver tail held high like he is doing a dressage show.

The pony soon realizes that he is being watched
And does the most magnificent rear as he kicks his front legs out.
He then gathers up more energy and does the loudest neigh
                                        anyone has ever heard.
Getting back onto all four hooves, he does a rearing, bucking canter
                                        to his water trough.

As he literally drops his head into the water, he tastes the cool
                                        freshness of it
And he knows this is good water and he must drink more.
After the pony has had his fill, he splashes the water around with
                                        his mouth,
Then he takes his head out of the trough.

He is feeling rather lonely until he hears the gate clang open.
When he realises it's his brother and his mother, he is so happy.
He prances and dances until he is joined by his family.
They all playfully rear up, greeting each other and blowing gently
                                        down each other's nostrils.

He suddenly looks up, seeing his owner looking at him.
He canters over to her as she holds her hand out in the air.
He pushes his nose into the palm of her hand and he feels the
                                        warmth of it.

As though greeting her, he rubs his face down hers and gives out
a chuckling neigh.
She then puts her hand into her pocket and pulls out a mint.
She holds it out to him and he gently takes it and bites into it.
As she walks away, he gives her a final neigh and trots back to his
mother and brother.

He leads them under the apple tree
Where they all lie down and rest.
But the main thing is he is happy and no longer alone.

Emily Tomlinson
Codsall Community High School

The Sky

The sky is so magical,
With its bright blue patches hiding behind huge clouds.
When in a mood, it explodes with bright white lights;
And the air is filled with low rumbling sounds.

The sky looks so close,
Like I could reach out and pet it like a dog to calm it down.
When it's still it's like a big piece of material protecting the Earth,
Anxiously hovering in case of danger.

When it finds that danger it drops
Falling closer and closer towards the Earth.
Getting darker and darker as it makes its descent.
Then as suddenly as it started falling,
It stops and the outside world is black.

Now the sky is filled with many stars,
Twinkling like someone smiling,
Showing us that it has filled its true potential.
Now the sky can rise again and guard the Earth from danger.

Jessica Green (14)
Codsall Community High School

Poison Boy

Curly brown locks, chestnut eyes
Tall, dark, olive skin, I was hooked on you
Like an alcoholic on
Red wine.

You were the stillness of Van Gogh before he
Painted the yellow vortex on his last sun.
You were the spider that lured me
Into your silk web.

You had everything sorted, everyone in line
You were my altar, my pride
Perfection you were, beauty to my eyes
Like freshly cut diamonds on a newly
Wed bride.

Entangled in your sweet fantasy you were
The ivy that muffled my ears.
Along the way I'd lose my faith
And you'd be there to mould me like clay.

All I really needed was you, but
Like a serpent you strangled my lungs.
Grasped my iced heart and melted it
In your warm hands.
I was torn to fight myself in two
To please your desires.

You were a last petal
Upon my dying red rose.
Butterfly with a broken wing,
I fly away.
You were never
Meant to be with me.

Anastasia Hunt (15)
Codsall Community High School

Friends

If friends were money I'd have none,
My happy days are surely gone.
I've just broken up with my best friend,
Yet she said our friendship would never end.
It was just because of a silly row,
I regret it - I feel lonely now.
I'm missing her, is she missing me?
I didn't realise how sad a girl could be!
I'll ask her tomorrow, I'll ask her at school,
Are we mates? Are we all cool?
Tomorrow has arrived, I get to school,
Now she's got other friends and I feel a fool.
After a while we decided to chat,
I've now got my friend back, but that's not that.
There's not only two of us anymore,
There's me, Laura, Stacey and friends galore.

Leanne Ewing (13)
Darlaston Community Science College

Hallowe'en Poem

On the 31st October you'd better be scared,
Goblins and ghouls rise from the dead, so be prepared,
Beware of the vampire's deadly bite,
So look in every place in sight,
Witches grasp broomsticks tight,
As they soar in the ebony light,
The scary, spooky sounds
That lurk on the misty grounds,
Frankenstein groans a mournful song,
As there are things that have gone wrong.
So be careful when you go to bed,
Because the next thing you know is you'll be *dead!*

Sophie Ward (11)
Darlaston Community Science College

I Wish . . .

I wish I could live in the sea,
but my breath wouldn't be helping me.
I wish I could be a millionaire,
but I really, really hate to share.
I wish I could be a celebrity,
but that isn't my speciality.
I wish I could live in Spain,
but that would bring my family pain.
I wish I could be an actress,
but I think I'd be under a lot of stress.
I wish I could be a presenter,
but I don't think that's really an adventure.
I wish I could be a pop star,
but I guess I'd have to live far.
I wish I could grab a cloud,
but I don't think that is allowed.
I wish I could help the poor,
but it doesn't help with another war.
I wish I could be a famous poet,
but that's up to you isn't it?

Nisha Rai (14)
Darlaston Community Science College

Hallowe'en

H aunted moon swayed across the sky.
A ncient stars sparkled in the darkness.
L ife is dead in the eyes of the graveyard.
L ightning rocks the gravestones.
O h so scary as the night draws on.
W ind positioned the trees like claws.
E bony skies fly across the world.
E ver hearing the noises of ghosts calling.
N asty fears await you.

Sharn Richards (11)
Darlaston Community Science College

Spooky Poem

Here I am,
At the alley in the dead of night.
I had better go or else,
The shadows might give me a fright.
I hear footsteps in the distance,
Creeping over here.
I'm very scared because,
My bravery is mere.
Huh, what's that?
It sounds like the closing of a door,
Or maybe somebody dropping dead on the floor.
Boy, am I in trouble,
I'd better get out of here.
Argh!

Daniel Morgan (11)
Darlaston Community Science College

Larry The Loafer

Larry the loafer
Was in a church
Singing a hymn
When someone threw
A tomato at him.

Tomatoes are soft
And don't hurt the skin
But this one did
It was in a tin!

Jacob Haskett (13)
Darlaston Community Science College

Spooky Poem

Its eyes glow in the dark,
It's black as the night sky,
A liquid pours out of its mouth,
As I begin to cry, 'Help me! Help me! Somebody help me!'
But nobody comes.
It gets ready to pounce,
Jump! It springs,
It licks my face,
What? Oh, it's just my Labrador, Max,
What a silly dog!

Shaun Hyde (12)
Darlaston Community Science College

Hallowe'en Has Begun

It was a dark ebony night,
No light in sight.

The trees grabbing,
Sharp and stabbing.

The stars shone,
Hallowe'en has begun!

The full moon golden-brown,
There's still no sound.

The air crisp with envy,
The leaves whirling with energy.

Natalie Phipps (11)
Darlaston Community Science College

Hallowe'en

Hallowe'en is very fun!
Trick or treating for everyone!
I love Hallowe'en, 'cause of the sweets!
Bet you love all your special treats!
The headless knight and all the ghosts,
All they do is boast and boast!
Nothing can frighten me I say,
That's true you know (my best friend), Faye!
I always say goodbye to the moon,
But I never ever say it that soon.
So every night I'll hear noises,
Saying things like, 'I'm stealing your voices!'

Taslima Begum Ali (11)
Darlaston Community Science College

Wolves

The gold and black army never fail,
They always win, either rain or hail.
One after the other the goals keep coming,
All the men outside are drumming.
All the fans are cheering their names,
While they watch all the games.
In the stands the crowds all cheer,
While they are sipping beer.
After the match the fans all riot,
But five minutes before they are quiet.

Aron Adams (13)
Darlaston Community Science College

I Wish

I wish I had a puppy dog,
A sheep dog would be best,
But not as cool
To take to school
As a bird who's lost its nest.

I wish I had a centipede,
So I could count its feet,
I'd like a cat,
I'd like a rat,
That really would be neat.

I wish I had a puppy dog,
I wish I had a horse,
With a guinea pig,
I'd dance a jig,
Yes, beauty is a horse, of course.

I wish I had a parrot,
I wish I had a mouse,
Or a slippery snake,
Which I would take,
On journeys round the house.

I wish, I wish,
I wish I had a pet,
A pet,
A pet,
A friend you can't forget.

Debbie Smith (12)
Darlaston Community Science College

Trick Or Treat

T onight it's Hallowe'en
R eady for a scream
 I n the darkness we all walk
C rooked house in sight
K nock on the door I do

O ld lady answers
'R atty kids,' she murmurs

 T wenty pence each
'R ight, clear off. Don't come back.'
 E ach ungrateful of her giving
 A way we run
 T o the streets full of treats.

Amy Hancocks (11)
Darlaston Community Science College

Rainbow

Pink, blue, purple, red
My mom had said.
Orange, yellow and green
Are the colours I have seen.
Black, white, grey, brown,
In my eyes it's like a crown.
I looked out of the window to see
And my face lit up with glee.

Jodie Steadman (13)
Darlaston Community Science College

Trick Or Treat 2

T wo ghosts linger in the darkness
R eady to scare us out of our skin
I nto the dark we step
C ould have been in our warm beds
K icking the ghosts as we go

O ne hasn't got a head
R ing, ring, goes the doorbell

'T rick or treat?' I say
'R uddy old kids,' I hear from the lady
''E re's 10p'
A nd away we run
T onight is a night I want to forget.

Bridie Ellis (11)
Darlaston Community Science College

Sunset

S unburnt-orange, ruby-red and glittering gold spread across the sky.
U nending colour from the corner of my eye.
N ow the colour is fading, the sun is going home.
S unset disappearing, all I see is a dome.
E nding far too fast.
T omorrow, hope it'll last.

Kirandeep Kaur (11)
Darlaston Community Science College

Supply Teacher

It's great when you've got a supply teacher
You go into lesson really late
Then when you have to give an excuse
See how much she can take.

She gives you a lecture
On how she will never come to this school again
And she tells you how much you have let your school down
Then here comes the class clown
We all grin but the teacher frowns.

He gets into trouble and gives a false name
We all know it's a game
The lesson's nearly over but our paper's blank
Then in comes the headmaster like an army tank.

The game is over, no more tic-tacs to play
But it's no fun for us as we have to stay
The supply teacher walks out with a cheesy grin
Laughs and says, 'Now look who has to stay in!'

Stacey Allwood (13)
Darlaston Community Science College

Racism

This is becoming a big threat in the world,
Kids getting hurt for no reason,
Millions of 'em each season,
Just cos of the colour of their skin,
I say chuck that BNP pamphlet in the bin,
This is like a war,
Next thing someone's out on the floor,
There's one question,
Why all this hate?
Can't we just have a debate?

Simran Singh (13)
Darlaston Community Science College

Best Friends

Friends, friends, are always there,
Wherever you look, they're there to care.
You can rely, you can depend,
Cos they are there, until the end.

Friends, friends, make you laugh,
They never say 'no, it's naff'.
You can be happy, you can be sad,
Because they will never ever turn bad.

Friends, friends, always support,
Even if you ended with a bad report.
They are there, so don't worry,
Don't you dare rush off in a hurry.

Friends, friends, are always there,
Wherever you look, they're there to care.
You can rely, you can depend,
Cos they are there, until the end.

Minakshi Neelam Samrai (13)
Darlaston Community Science College

Scared!

S omeone screaming next door!
C ar doors slamming shut!
A cry from down the ally!
R adios on full blast!
E veryone's scared!
D ogs barking in the streets!

Stacey Slater (11)
Darlaston Community Science College

Bugs, Bugs

Spider, spider,
In its web,
Spider, spider,
Caught a fly again.

Ants, ants,
Crawling along,
Ants, ants,
All humming a song.

Beetle, beetle,
Scurry away,
Beetle, beetle,
Keeping at bay.

Bugs, bugs,
Everywhere,
Bugs, bugs,
In your hair!

Luke Pitcher (13)
Darlaston Community Science College

Wrestling

This was the greatest day
I went to see some wrestling
I went to see my favourite sport
And my favourite wrestler, Sting.

This was my favourite day
This was the greatest time
Sting was in the main event
I thought the world was mine.

It was a good match
Even though he lost
Sting put up a great fight
It was worth the cost.

James Seymour (13)
Darlaston Community Science College

Loving You

Loving you is easy,
Letting go is hard,
Even though you know I love you,
We are still apart.

My love for you goes higher,
Than any star,
My love for you if you threw it as a ball,
Would go far.

Your love for me
Is non-existent,
Your love for me is nothing,
We are very distant.

Our love for each other
Is meaningless,
If I love you but you love beauty
And that I do not possess.

My heart you broke,
My tears you made fall,
All because . . .
I love *you*.

Fiona Mason (13)
Darlaston Community Science College

A Dedication To My Family

F orever you stand by my side,
A nd all the time I need you, you're there,
M orning to night I love you,
 I f I ever need help, I know you'll always be there,
L ove isn't good enough for you lot,
Y ou lot mean the world to me.

Lauren Pedley (11)
Darlaston Community Science College

My Smashin' Mate

No one could replace you,
As if they ever would,
You're always there, you always care,
You're my smashin' bestest bud.

You're always there for me,
Here through good and bad,
Even when I'm lonely,
And especially when I'm sad.

You're so sweet,
You're such a treat,
Even when I'm alone,
You're always there to comfort me
              or call me on the phone.

That's why you're my smashin' mate,
So I wrote this poem for you,
I love you like a sister,
I hope you feel the same way too.

Sonia Lal (13)
Darlaston Community Science College

Sadness

Sadness is the colour of grey,
It smells like a wet dog,
It tastes like mushy peas,
It looks like a dead rat
And it sounds like people arguing.
Sadness is the worst thing,
It makes you feel tired all the while,
It also smells like a dirty sewer
And tastes like Brussels sprouts,
Plus it looks like hideous creatures like spiders.

Emma Brookes (11)
Darlaston Community Science College

Anne Frank

I wish I could leave and run away far,
My life is so different just because I wear a star.
Even though I'm a Jew,
Am I any different from you?
Inside I'm full of anger and rage,
I feel like a dog locked up in a cage.
I can't walk the streets after 8 o'clock,
Or visit the cinema wearing my best frock.
I'm sick of these Germans thinking they own the place,
They loathe and despise me because of my race.
Sometimes I think it's all gonna stop,
But then I hear another bomb drop.
How can the Germans cause so much pain?
Is it the right thing to do for personal gain?
I want to shout that I'm Jewish and I'm proud,
But I might be murdered for being too loud.
When I wake up tomorrow, I want this all to end,
I thank you pen and paper for being my only friend.

Chaumét Kenton (13)
Deansfield High School

The Door

Go and open the door
Go and have a tour
There may be something you haven't seen before
There might be a dog on roller skates
There might be a cat on the gate
So go and open the door
And see something you haven't seen before
Like a granny kicking a ball
Or a baby so tall
So go and open the door
Go and open the door
Go and open the door.

Laura Pitt (12)
Deansfield High School

Misery

Kitty's the only friend I've got
I care for her and love her a lot
I wish my family would try and see
They say they love me but then let me be
I write to Kitty every day
'How very stupid!' my brother says
They just don't know how sad I am
My brother, my pa or even my mam
The Germans hate us, I know they do
All of this because I'm a Jew
We have to be secretive, careful and quiet
Or else the Germans may start a riot
I used to be scared
But no one cared
It's no different today
Or any other day
But I'll always remember, Kitty's my friend
And she'll be there until the very end.

Leigh Thomas (13)
Deansfield High School

Troubled!

Life under German rule is so unfair,
we aren't even allowed to cross the square.
It's like my freedom has been torn apart,
it feels like someone has broken my heart.
As I write this, my teardrops fall,
all I have to look at are four plain walls.
We're forbidden on trams, we have to turn in our bikes,
Jews and Germans are always getting into fights.
All I wish is for the world to be at peace,
all my sadness I wish I could release.
No one understands what this is like for me,
I only wish I could make them see.
I have no one to love, no one to be near,
I wish someone could see me through this first year.
So you see, Kitty is my only friend
and I know she'll be with me until the end.

Stacey Williams (13)
Deansfield High School

The Door

Go and open the door
There is a man on a tour
There's a man with a gun
Looking for his son.

Go and open the door
There is a man with a straw
'Give me a drink'
Hang on, let me think.

Go and open the door
There's a man asking for more
'There's a long walk ahead of you
I would like some stew.'

Go and open the door
There's a German asking for war
'I challenge you to a war'
The door is shut forever and ever.

Guisseppi Silba (11)
Deansfield High School

My Life

My life is a dark, cold, poisoned world.
It's filled with hatred and bigotry
Disapproving rules that hurt me
Neither laughter nor joy has come to me
Since those ignorant, selfish animals invaded our families.

My life is a cage with iron bars surrounding my freedom.
I long to walk the streets with no one watching over me
Verbal abuse coming from ear to ear.
It makes me feel unwanted.
It makes me fear.

I want the world to hear my plea.
'Please come and help me'
This world is too dangerous and it feels like I'm in Hell.
But if I never had faith I wouldn't be alive still.
I would give my soul to God to make things right.
But God's watching over me
So I'm alright.

I appreciate God for letting me survive
I appreciate God because He's my life.

Autumn Anderson (13)
Deansfield High School

Anne Frank Poem

Anne Frank was a lonely girl,
She felt like she was in her own world.
Everything she tried to do,
She couldn't because she was a Jew.
She couldn't go to the cinemas because it wasn't allowed,
The reason for this was the German crowd.
She only had one special friend,
Who was with her since the beginning to end.
This was her diary,
Her one true friend,
She couldn't take the suffering and the pain.
If she heard one more gunshot she'd go insane,
This is her life,
Full of troubles and strife.
She felt like leaning out of the window
And saying, 'I'm a Jew and I'm proud.'
Why was she and all the Jews treated this way?
She just wished it would end one day.

Simone Campbell (13)
Deansfield High School

No Hopes, No Dreams

Before this painful vain
I was a young sweet girl without any shame
But now I live in a cage
Every day is a thick blank page

I am only a Jew
Therefore, I must stay true
Without strength and determination
I will not get through this hatred nation

Germans rule the world I live in
I have no control of what they are thinking
I wish I could go back to the girl I was
Where freedom was with me and the Germans were lost

I remember a time when
I didn't have to care
I could fly high in the sky
With time passing me by

But my hopes and dreams
Are all forgotten now
There's not much I can do
But to lay on the ground

But at least I'm still breathing
At least I'm not dead
There's only one thing to do now
To lie down in my bed.

Sara Thompson (14)
Deansfield High School

Stuck

I am stuck
I have no luck
I'm in my house
Caged up like a mouse
I can't go out
It's half-past eight
It's getting late
It's nearly nine
Time for my bath
That's always a laugh
I need to go to bed
To rest my head
Time to say bye
Doesn't time fly
I'll see you tomorrow
That's if I'm still alive
Life is unpredictable since these German's took over our lives.

Adam Ajchinger (13)
Deansfield High School

The Poem Of Anne

Anneliese is my full name,
I am not to blame.
Some days I wish that I was dead,
These are the words that are going round in my head.

The events that happened I regret and hate,
It was so hard to work and concentrate.
Living under Germans' rule,
I think this is so, so cruel.

I get so lonely,
This camp doesn't feel homely.
Looking at sad faces,
Rarely around I never see a smile put in places.

I want to go to the swimming baths,
All that the Germans do is look and laugh.
Anyone in my situation would think that life is so unfair,
Kitty, my diary, the only true friend who cares.

Some days I get so bored,
I sit there praying to the Lord.
All that I do is sit in my attic and cry,
Thinking of that day when I am going to die.

Nichola Patrick (13)
Deansfield High School

Anne Frank

A nne is my name and I am not to blame
N early all the Jews need to be in shame
N obody cares about me or you
E verything I do has to be with a Jew

F amily now is all I have
R emembering all the trouble I have
A nd nobody cares about me or you
N ow only because I'm a Jew
K itty is my diary and is my friend who is true

J ealous Germans just want us to say, 'Boo hoo'
E veryone around me I cannot trust
W hen Germans are around me I feel like I've combust.

Anne Frank she's Jewish.

Letish Fisher (13)
Deansfield High School

Anne Frank - The Poem

The Jews have no life under German rule,
I hate life being so uncool.
My next-door neighbour was killed last night,
It gave me and my family such a fright.
I'm going to keep a diary and I'm calling it Kitty,
I'm going to write about the Germans, thinking they are witty.

In my diary I'm going to give it to you straight,
About those Germans and their loathing and hate.
Because of their rules I'm trapped in my home,
I want to go up to a German and have a great moan
Whenever the Germans see my face,
They look at me as if I'm a disgrace.

In my body there should be a great soul,
But instead there's just a huge, gaping hole.
Hiding from the Germans is such a terrible life,
The village should be like it used to be, without the death or strife.
They have guns and bombs beyond our imagination,
Their weapons of mass destruction have shook our whole nation.

I don't know why Adolf Hitler wants to start a war,
But know that this kind of thing has happened before.
And that is where my story ends,
About the Germans, the Jews, my life and my friends.

Richard Burns (14)
Deansfield High School

My Dinosaur Friend

I was looking out my window when I heard a great roar,
A dinosaur in my back garden, 20ft tall.
He walked up and down the yard, all worried and sad,
I asked him, 'What's the matter, it can't be all bad?'

He told me he was lost from his overcrowded herd,
He was distracted for a moment by a beautifully coloured bird.
His family were adventurous and travelled all the time,
His father was a champion fighter, back in his prime.

I asked him if he'd like to stop and have a bite to eat,
As he came through the door he fell over his two huge feet.
Mom came in and asked me what was wrong,
I said, 'Nothing Mom, when is dinner done? I hope it's not too long.'

We went up to my room and played on my games console,
I put in one of my favourites where you had to find and beat
the killer mole.
When it was time for him to go we heard his family call,
He jumped up in the air with glee; he'd found his family once
and for all.

Daniel Whittaker (13)
Deansfield High School

Trapped In My Own Home

Jewish people treated inconsiderately,
Just because we're different,
I'm trapped unwillingly!

I want to run away as far as I can,
To get out of this hellhole,
That I would be banned,
Deep down in my soul,
I know Hitler's to blame,
Because of him I am not the same.

I have to walk, stand and stare,
Just because of a star I wear,
I now can feel this horrid, harmful pain,
This unsatisfying shame,
To those I plea,
To let me go and be myself and just be free!

For once I know in my heart
This world, and people
Are tearing me apart,
Nothing I can do
To make them change
Because of this I feel ashamed.

Germans look down at us,
To get their enjoyment,
They spit and shout verbal abuse,
Just to start an argument.
Others join in and start to say,
'Get your religion out of this place!
You're nothing but dirt, so go back home,
With your disgrace you're sure to be alone!'

Claire Lane (13)
Deansfield High School

My Feelings Of Life

The trees and grass
They grow before I finish a glass
I tidy my room
I can't wait to meet my groom
I'm looking forward to my wedding
Before I knew it I was yelling
My heart pumps fast
I would hate another task
The light seems bright, but it's night
I went to sit on a stool
Before I knew it, I was back at school
Another boring day
I may as well get married in May
My teacher says
'Kayla, don't look out the window, I know it's double glazed'
I moved through life again
It's not what I dreamt
I should not have believed
That's my feelings
I won't stop healing
I'm the girl who shares her heart today.

Michayla Mallinson (13)
Deansfield High School

The Tiger

Vicious, jagged claws,
Glowing, green eyes,
A scary, strong set of jaws,
The tiger is out on the prowl tonight.

His tail is swishing,
Curved, camouflage stripes,
A strong, gleaming body,
The tiger is on the move.

Moving stealthily through the undergrowth
With his coat bathed in moonlight,
Silently padding through the grass,
Waiting to pounce . . .

> . . . be careful . . .
> . . . he's coming . . .
> . . . *gotcha!*

Joanne Johnson (11)
Deansfield High School

Riding On White Sands

Sun was beating down upon me,
Sea lapping at my horse's hooves.
Like a cold, icy hand stroking the beach
The sun dazzling my eyes
His coat gleaming in the early morning sun
Gentle thudding of hooves in the soft, white sand
U-shaped hoof prints left behind
To be washed up by the sea
Wind streaming in our hair
Snorting and neighing of my trusty steed
Excited feelings
Swift movements of the horse's legs
Relaxing
Peaceful
Riding off into the beautiful sunrise.

Katie Weston (11)
Hagley Middle School

The Dragon

It appeared from the mist throwing darkness around it,
A tyrannical dragon with scales like fire,
Piercing eyes cut into my soul,
His teeth gleaming like ivory,
Look down to his talons,
Capable of splitting boulders,
Rocks and dirt tumbled off the sheer edge of a once gleaming,
                                                    white cliff,
Flame to melt steel flickered out of his snout when he flinched,
Lightning struck and the fiend roared,
His wings fanned open,
Swiftly, silently, he began to take flight,
The beast cut through the darkness like a knife through butter,
As he flew around,
Swooped down to me . . .

Charles Hughes (12)
Hagley Middle School

Busy London Street

Street packed with bodies like sardines in a tin
Traffic lights changing colour every second
People cramming into shops
Jackhammers vibrating in your head
Toes getting flattened by people's feet
Cars slowly crawling down the road
Furious shouting down the crowded street
Car horns piercing your ears
Bodies banging into each other.

Matthew Wood (11)
Hagley Middle School

Desert Island Dreams

The sun beats down,
Baking the sand,
Shells dazzle like jewels,
Sinking into soft sands,
As they are washed calmly upon the waterside.

Lizards clamber up golden palms,
Fuzzy coconuts drop,
Like leaves off a tree,
Scaly snakes writhe up tough, rough boughs,
Jeering slyly at all who pass.

Aqua water laps serenely on pearl-white shores,
Sky like a vast ocean,
With drifting clouds like silent shoals of fish,
Breeze whistling,
Trees shivering,
As the sun sinks into the distance . . .

Rebecca Priest (11)
Hagley Middle School

Egyptian Dunes

Bitter sand grates Hathor's skin,
Cold morning dwells in starlight.
Tears of Isis in azure depths,
Half-human shadows ripple at night.

Morning past and sandaled toes step out into the glare.
The omniscient eye perceiving
Horus on his heavenly throne,
Rolling the sun across the sky alone.

Distant, smouldering orange burning to embers.
Light embraces black.
Crimson skies cast shadows over day and calm waters,
Stealing daylight away to tomorrow
And in darkness Lord Anubis brings toil and sorrow.

Shellyane Bryan (16)
King Edward VI College

Work Will Set You Free

A road with no signs, a wall with no end,
A gate with the words:
'Work Will Set You Free'.

Finely dressed, suitcases at hand,
A face full of delight,
David's children walk.

Into the courtyard, around a corner,
A broken cross displayed,
Prison awaits them all.

Belongings removed, identities proved,
One desperate display of despair,
What fate lies ahead?

An undesirable world, where work entails,
To walk, and walk, and walk,
A circle to freedom.

Until at last!

A walk downhill, where walls surround,
Stood in front of logs,
Bang, bang, bang . . .
    . . . then not another sound.

Or a walk uphill, into the showers,
A man with Godly powers,
No water but short of breath . . .
    . . . engulfed by death.

Into a room, to join the others,
This is the freedom earned:
An eternity of sleep.

Lucinda Russell (16)
King Edward VI College

The Coast Of Dorset/Lulworth, Southern England

She took up her brush against the sky
And from the bands of grey,
Spilled bands of blue, indigo and gold
Creating the sky in her sway.
She turned her hand upon the sea
And pondered its fluid grace.
She made it clear to reflect the sky
And the moon that she gave her face.

She looked around upon the scene,
With mild calculation.
The hills, they were rolling, serene and calm.
As was the placid ocean.
Lacking all lustre, she made a change,
With divine indiscrimination,
She enraged the seas and the hills she did tease,
Shaking the earth to its ancient foundations.

Though tumultuous was the design,
The aftermath was inspiring!
The hills lay bent above towers of stone,
And wizened arches were stood in the raising.
The landscape was scarred,
And in regard, the winds sang bitter lament.
Sounding through the arches, which to her power
Stood frightful testament.

With her body she had laid down the soil
And with her hands had begun to work.
With the sea she sculpted the land mass,
Made craters for creatures to lurk.
She later considered her creation,
And in according with its worth,
Looked down upon it and smiled
Giving the sun its mirth.

God is an artist,
As the coast of Dorset know well.
How she etched her name into every cliff face,
Poured her soul into every well.
She shared with the sea her laughter,
And with the waves her artisan hands,
To work their magic upon the coast,
To shape its twisting sands.

Dale Kedwards (16)
King Edward VI College

Darkness

Vulnerable and alone,
Feelings are intense,
With nowhere to turn,
No direction or sense.

Darkness filters everywhere,
Blacker than black,
Swallowing the light,
In every corner and crack.

The aching of loneliness,
Waiting to be found,
The silence is deafening,
There is no other sound.

Eyes sting with passion,
An immense feeling grows,
To spot a wandering saviour,
As hope starts to show.

The darkness gets thicker,
Suffocating within,
Trapped in the nightmare,
The place is a sin.

Kerry Pinches (16)
King Edward VI College

Chattering Castle Of False Fear

Time cuts and carves and chips away
As my sanity starts to rot,
The thought is unthinkable,
The fear is palpable,
The time's one I wish it not.

The whitewashed walls consume me,
Decay my will to stay,
I hate this place as scissors to rock
And yet I'm here again, sitting, waiting, watching the seconds tick,
Tick-tock.

'Why?' I ask myself. 'Why am I here once more?'
With the white aproned man
And the nurse by the door? And the line of instruments
Grinning at me, as I swallow my pride
And wish to be, anywhere else
But this torturous place, as I question
Why my pulse starts to race.

And, as his eyes drill in to mine,
I'm greeted with a sparkling smile,
I brace myself to the seat, and, instantly admit . . . defeat.

Caroline Davis (16)
King Edward VI College

Summer In The Park

As the day goes by the shadows move slowly all around,
Not a sound to be heard,
Just the grass,
Rustling all over the ground.

Occasionally the orange and yellow flicker of the sun,
Looks like a bed of roses come undone.
Children running everywhere,
However, not a slight sound or evil glare.

The park is a place for everyone:
Friends, and families, but they seem to have all gone.
Today is the quietest it's ever been,
It really is like nothing I've seen.

Then all of a sudden, I snap out of this dream,
Everything around changes back to the real scene.
Now there's me, you and everyone,
All the fantasies I had . . . dead and gone.

Sarah Hazelwood (16)
King Edward VI College

A Place In Time

Frustration ebbs and flows
Like the sands of wasted time
Invisible clocks - tick-tock, tick-tock
Inside the mind's confine
In a rut
To sit? To stand? To jump, or fall?
To wait for something more?
What to do within this place?
To yet remain unsure.

Joe Stone (16)
King Edward VI College

England

England is a place I know
I've lived here all my life
There are a lot of single men
All looking for a wife.

It rains a lot and snows sometimes
The weather's pretty bad
Some people like the rain
But it just makes me sad.

When it's hot it's very hot
Everyone heads for the beach
When it's cold we stay at home
Some cook, some clean, some teach.

England is a busy place
With pubs and clubs and bars
And traffic wardens on the street
Where people park their cars.

Josie Adams (17)
King Edward VI College

Serene Dream

Jet rolls me under the waves,
A darkness graphically illuminated with colour,
Images dance through the empty pages,
Subconscious fears in a timeless expanse.
Here I'm empowered or hiding away,
Whoever I'm choosing to be.
As the warm lethargy twinkles its last,
A dying star in a time long forgotten,
Red sears, tranquillity is lost.

Sophie Wythes (16)
King Edward VI College

The Maldivian Sea

The Maldivian Sea
So colourful and bright
I watch the amazing display
Performed by the fish
Especially for me.

The fish by the reef
So peaceful and serene
As I watch them
I drift into another world
And lose all track of time.

Baby sharks
Seeming so scary and yet so sweet
Puffa fish
That blow up like balloons
Whenever I go near.

When I bring my head out of the water
It all seems like a dream
Until I put my head back down
And re-enter that wonderful world below.

Claire Lewis (16)
King Edward VI College

Osbourne Bay

Still on the water, not a wave in sight,
The solid surface of land could not feel more stable.
Flecks of light, ripple and reflect on the blue hull,
Sails in, not moving, desert quiet.
Breeze washes over the land's empty beaches,
And the two towers peering over the trees.

Sophie Gower (16)
King Edward VI College

Feelings

With this feeling inside
This feeling I hide
For the place I long to go
The place I long to go

I used to dream, dream of it every night
A solemn silence, nothing to be heard, but the beating of my heart
Calling tears from deep inside
The pictures, the memories I try to hide
Kept locked up within my mind
Of the place I long to go
The place I long to go

Of late it's been hard to go inside
Knowing in my heart I cannot go where I long to
In my mind, in my head, I've been there a million times
But my body has yet to travel that distance that journey yet
                            to be completed

Of that place I long to go
That place I long to go

The thoughts, the feelings, the dreams
Of the place I long to go

And that place I long to go . . . that's for me to know.

Carly Snead (16)
King Edward VI College

In Memory Of

The serenity of complacency
The mark of true childhood
This inner peace
It does not define me
But it reminds me of
That place I used to know
I loved to go
To stand and observe the world
(Or so I thought)
From this secret perch
Do not disturb
Birdsong announces those obvious thieves
Landing in the rhubarb patch
Pilfering damsons from the tree
Pungent oil emanates from the shed
Still I stand
Alone and at home
Safe in the knowledge that
This is a place I will always come back to
In memories and dreams
That forfeit the years that have passed
Embedded in me
Locked away, a comfort zone
To retreat to from the mayhem
Where I can stand and relax
The shed will fall down
The rhubarb will flail
The green grass will fade to yellow
The tree will stand
Alone and at home
And I will go back
To stand beside the only survivor.

Stacey Davies (16)
King Edward VI College

Child's View Of The City

The blue balloon danced and waltzed against the sky,
As we lay against the last knotted grey tree,
In the knotted grey city.

We filled our eyes with the orange burns,
As the sun grew heavy and died,
In its last evening sunrise,
And held hands.

Towers of silver crashed against the breadth of the heavens,
And the rushing cars and mechanical people tore the city apart,
The noise was rushing, crashing, searingly soothing,
But as the light came on, and the sun turned off,
The sky donned a black veil of stars,
Which fitted it like a wedding dress,
And we both proclaimed it the most beautiful sight in the world.

Somewhere in the mechanical wilderness,
A car alarm scarred the surface of our silence,
A crying child sang the requiem of our moment,
The tower blocks declared their power over us,
And a single blue balloon danced and waltzed against the sky.

The forty thousand men and women slipped into sleep,
As, one by one, light after light bore the brunt,
And faded away,
Until we sat alone under the light of the knotted grey tree,
Burning into the ground,
And the city was complete.

The important men of the city chuckled a fat, wealthy chuckle,
                                        raised their top hats,
And sank into the cracks which lined the streets with a bow
                                        and a wave,
The traffic lights bowed their heads and cried tears of red, amber
                                        and green,
The fires of the moving industry licked the buildings and towers
                                        with tongues of discord,
And we saw the wealth we hold so dearly become nothing more
                                        than paper and metal.

We walked through the waste,
And found no sign of the trees and flowers we held so dear,
And we never noticed,
The towers of grey,
The mechanical people,
The tearing vehicles,
The laughing people,
Crushed to death under the weight of one single blue balloon,
Dancing and waltzing against the stagnant sky.

Jack Del-Vecchio (17)
King Edward VI College

In This Fading Place

In this place
The skies are made of gold
The sun drifts slowly away
Behind the faintest of clouds.

In this place
Fields of nothing watch every move
The soft touch of echoing memories
Horses galloping in the softest winds.

In this place
Beauty is a distant queen
She softly touches the shadows
Of your smallest, wildest dreams.

In this place
Someone forgot to watch the views
In this place
For me, you are fading far too soon.

Sam Brett (16)
King Edward VI College

At The Football Ground

At the football ground,
The fans they roar,
Two pounds, ten a pint,
One for ever goal we score.

At the football ground,
The fans they jump,
Listen to their hearts,
You can hear the adrenaline pump.

At the football ground,
The fans they cheer,
Whilst waving their scarves,
If we don't win, we'll be back next year.

At the football ground,
I love to shout,
Looking through my eyes,
Supporting your team is what it's all about.

Jenna Evans (16)
King Edward VI College

Meditation

The sun shines high in the sky,
The Great Orb up above shines blissfully down,
Gloriously coating all that are underneath.
Along this long shore gentle waves lap upon the sand,
Mere echoes of their former glory.

The sand whips along with the breeze.
The fish swim.
The trees sway,
The crabs scuttle.
The birds soar.
The waves crash.
And all is peaceful underneath.

Jimmy Martin (16)
King Edward VI College

The Landscape In My Head

The stars light a path through the shroud of black velvet,
I follow the moon, my ethereal guide,
So when my eyes close and my mind drifts completely,
I walk through the gates and then vanish inside . . .

I hear nothing more than the echo of faint whispers
That dance on the wind, and tease my ears to listen.
No jagged-edged scream pierces the stillness like lightning,
And no thundering bellow engulfs the air.

I see the inky-black night above me, dotted with chalky full stops.
I become driftwood on the ocean of the world below me,
Far above the seabed, I never want to dive in again,
And drown in my worry and fear and unease.

I smell dizzying aromas that make me remember, until
I cannot distinguish the present from the past:
A tidal wave of memories filling my head
Like a waterfall, cascading into my mind.

I feel like I am in a water colour painting:
Blurred around the edges, full of beauty and colour,
Surreal, tranquil and wondrous,
The world passes me by in my dreamland.

And then I am back in the harsh morning sunshine,
The cycle of living continues to turn,
But the place in my head is all I can think of,
And so I wait for the darkness, when I can return.

Hannah Webb (16)
King Edward VI College

The Void

Once again darkness reigns, nothing visible in sight,
Struggling and fighting, oh how you miss the light,
Where you were King, happiness swept over you,
You've been there before, yet it all seems so new.

Then you turn and can see
Once again you feel free
The joy of serendipity
To dreams you find the key.

Be a knight of the round table,
Be the hero of the day,
Be the star in your own fable,
Be whatever you can say.
Be a soldier of the people,
Be chased by an android,
Oh it all now seems so simple,
For you to fill the void.

Once again darkness reigns, have you been here before?
Oh the wonders you have seen, you wish to witness more.
Where you were King, happiness swept over you,
You've been there before, yet it all seems so new.

Turn again and you'll see,
How it feels to be free,
For this there is no fee,
To dreams you find the key.

Be the ruler of the day,
Be the master of the night,
Be the creator of the way,
Mustn't ever lose the light.
Be a teacher of the masses,
No more need to be annoyed,
Teach them all how it's so simple,
For them to fill the void.

A new darkness appears, much unlike the last,
Struggling and fighting, you escaped in the past.
That doesn't work here, a new day here unfurls,
You must wait until the next time, welcome back to the real world.

John Tyson (16)
King Edward VI College

The Melodious Guardian

The mysterious modern beauty faces her world
Full of words with no meaning but so much importance
Her being, split into two.
A thorn yet a rose and a sting with a stroke.

She catches the tears that fell on the bubble
And flings her arms around the wounded.
Our middle halves connected but,
We share so much more than a tag.

She strums away my pain
And makes my dark light.
The taunts that were flung fall out of sight,
But the angel that comforted stays in my heart.

One quarter of four, essential and wanted,
Her cog turns our wheels of spirals.
If only she knew the life that she's saved,
But for now kept a secret from my guardian who sings.

Luci Weaver (17)
King Edward VI College

In The Pits Of My Soul

At this place I discovered why the pen was born,
It was held bare before me, the need to commemorate the truth,
I found that it was within these pits of my soul,
Where I could denunciate those 'experts' in suits,
I discovered creativity and beauty,
In the space of a few words/lines,
Poems on truth, poems dedicated to you,
Poems written to appreciate the splendour of God's design,
From the pits of my soul,
I have discovered this place,
Where I can write and be who I am,
This is my domain, this is my space,

Let the pounding of the sea be an inspiration to others,
For me, the pounding of hearts is enough insight,
Clutching my memories and my hopes I stay rooted to this spot,
And let life drift by, eliminating ignorance with the truth as my light.

Shakeel Liaqat (17)
King Edward VI College

My Favourite Place

I am alone and in peace,
There is nothing troubling me,
Worries do not matter,
When I am here I am in my favourite place.

The world has stopped spinning,
The fast, furious, frantic cars are silent,
Everything around me is quiet,
At last I am alone and safe.

The hustle and bustle in the streets has stopped,
There is no pushing, pulling, screaming or swearing,
Just peace and tranquillity,
Just me in my favourite place.

My favourite place,
A place where only I can sit,
There are no long, loud arguments,
Just me alone and in peace.

Miriam Haynes (16)
King Edward VI College

Ups And Downs

Bowling
Pins crashing down
Raging rock music
Shouts and screams,
'I've won, I've won!'
Scrumptious chips, licking the salt off my lips.

Stinking, rotten cold
Streaming, stuffed nose
Closed in a box
Stuck
Trapped inside a dreary day
Golden, sunny summer outside.

Laura Brooks (14)
Penn Hall School

Yellow

Yellow is the yolk of fresh fried eggs
It is the taste of vanilla ice cream
It is the touch of a soft teddy bear
It is the sound of bells on a hot, sunny day
It is the sun lighting up the sky.

Katie Retallick (13)
Penn Hall School

Purple

Purple is the touch of my warm trousers
Purple is the smell of plums
Purple looks like Ribena in a glass
Purple sounds like blackcurrant juice pouring out of a bottle
Purple tastes like delicious grapes.

Harminder Nagra (13)
Penn Hall School

Blue

Blue is the bright, cloudless sky on a summer's day
It is the crashing waves splashing over pebbles
It is the fresh smell of bluebells in the wood
The tropical taste of a blueberry bar
The feel of a new, smooth, silky Albion shirt.

Alex Giles (13)
Penn Hall School

Ups And Downs

The Millennium Stadium
3-0 to Wolves
Throat raw from cheering
We've gone up!

New white boots
In a seaside shop
Forty pounds
'Too expensive,' Mom says
Disappointment!

Simon Jordan (15)
Penn Hall School

Red

Red is the taste of fresh, juicy strawberries
Red is the sound of loud sirens on a fire engine
Red is the raging flames of a fire
Red is the feeling of anger
Red is the smell of red roses.

Sam Harris (13)
Penn Hall School

Green

Green is fresh wet grass
It is the smell of fresh, minty herbs
It is the sharp, sour taste of lime juice
It is the feel of my favourite teddy
It is the sound of rustling leaves.

Jodie Willetts (13)
Penn Hall School

All She Ever Wanted

All she ever wanted
Was a family who'd be true
Someone who'd never do the things
Her parents used to do

All she ever dreamed of
Was to stop being sad
But most of all two people
She could call her mum and dad

All she ever needed
Were clean clothes upon her back
Warm food inside her stomach
No more dirt to turn her black

All she ever hoped for
Was a home where she felt right
A place to keep her warm
And to keep her safe at night

All she ever longed for
Was a sister or a brother
And all together they would play
And care for one another

All she ever wished for
Was that her future would be bright
To go to school like every child
And to learn to read and write

All she ever prayed for
Was to have a better life
And soon her prayers were answered
When she met with Jesus Christ

All she ever wanted
Was behind the Heaven's door
And as she was contented
She no longer wanted more

See Jesus had decided
She had suffered for too long
And with his power he changed this girl
From feeble into strong

He gave her all she wanted
Filled her heart up to the brim
And all because she never gave up
Having faith in Him.

Cassandra Hall-Alexander (14)
Perry Beeches School

Why Do People Die?

Why do people have to die and leave the people they love?
They just disappear and suddenly go, to the man above
Around the world people are dying
Leaving their family crying
Their tears fall down
Their smile is a frown
Why do people have to die?
People have no medical care
The people around just stand and stare
They don't help out, it's just a thing
They wait for an angel to spread its wings.
The angel sets the spirit free
And gives the spirit the ultimate key
The key to eternal happiness
The place where things are nice and fresh
When you get there you start a new life
You don't have to worry about the struggle and strife
You don't have to worry about the aches and pains
There are no more stormy days, no rain
You don't have to shed those sickening tears
'Cause you good people will soon be here.

Layla Samuda (14)
Perry Beeches School

Love Is . . .

Love is between you and me.
Love is bigger than a wide open sea.
Love is the way God made it to be,
Love is . . .

Love is a feeling so strong.
Love is the alternate bond.
Love is a sweet song,
Love is . . .

Love is a light so bright.
Love is the moon on a dark night.
Love is a great height,
Love is . . .

Love is happiness.
Love is made from many sounds.
Love is what makes the world go round!
Love is . . .

Annie Williams (14)
Perry Beeches School

Love Is . . .

Love is a rose that grows in the summer
Love is a fairy tale that never ends
Love is a sparkling stream that goes on forever
Love is something that could bring back revenge
Love is a dream, but could be a nightmare
But wherever you are
Or wherever you go
Your heart will carry on
And your love will grow and grow.

Danielle Billingham (14)
Perry Beeches School

Love

Love is when someone's on your mind 24/7
Love is when you feel like you're in Heaven
Love is a feeling so sweet and so fair
It's like that feeling so warm when nobody's there.
Love happens even straight away or at your own pace
It's something you see all over your face.
Love is so complicated yet so simple it seems
You can be so in love even in your dreams
Love is sunshine on a winter's day
You feel so happy even when you feel grey.
Love is mostly about trust and devotion
It's as if you've drunk a magic love potion.
Love also involves jealousy and war
You can feel such hatred, but don't know what for
Love is something you just can't ignore
You can't just leave those feelings rotting at the core.
When you find that right someone and look deep inside
You'll feel those feelings you just cannot hide.
Love is so pure, it's just like a dove
Hopefully we all will find *love*.

Victoria Jenkins (13)
Perry Beeches School

Where Is Love?

Love is found in the deepest of seas
Love is in the hearts of you and me.

Love is beautiful, soft and sleek
Love is a kiss on a baby's cheek.

Love is the wind whispering your name
I love you, I hope you feel the same.

The last thing I want to say won't rhyme
But please read it and take your time.

I dropped a tear in the ocean today
And when they find it I'll stop loving you.

Phylicia Jarrett (14)
Perry Beeches School

Alone

Being alone gives you time to think
Being alone can make your heart sink
Alone in the dark grieving
You may think of leaving.
Leaving the pain of this world behind
Is this all that's on your mind?
That life is not worth it!
But now you've found your light
Your spirit soars to new heights
You are glad for life
With no more strife
But do you miss that little feeling
Being alone, staring at the ceiling?

Hayley Allen (14)
Perry Beeches School

Teachers

Teachers are the bogeymen
Giving out detentions or referrals
Destroying young children's spirits in a flash
Yelling, 'Don't lie boy!' Or, 'I want the truth!'
All of them praying for the return of the cane
Then when the bell goes they melt
For on Saturday they can't terrorise children
But they set their evil accomplice - homework, on the victims
Then Judgement Day comes - commonly known as Monday.

Thomas Brannigan (13)
Perry Beeches School

Deprived

Tears I cry, but no one knows,
Sitting here full of woe,
Just me and the knife all alone.

How I feel is not what they see
I feel like a prisoner trapped out at sea.
What is this life if I can't have fun?
What is this life if I can't feel love?

I wish I could just drift away
To where the palm trees twirl and sway,
I wish I could just break the hold
That's holding me down, I'd love to be so bold.

When people around me laugh and joke,
It fills me with anger and makes me choke.
My mind is filled with broken memories
If only they would give me moments to cherish.

Melissa Callaghan (14)
Perry Beeches School

What Is Love?

Love is what we want it to be
Love is different for you and me

For me love is what makes the world go round
It's what makes a flower come out from under the ground
Love is the seasons in a year
Love is never having to fear.

Love is the feeling when summer wakes
Love is being there, no matter what it takes.

Paris Dawkins (13)
Perry Beeches School

Hate

Satan, Satan from down below,
Hate is not your friend, it is your foe.
Hate is bad, it makes me sad,
It makes me crazy and so mad.
Bring me love from up above,
Hate is not as beautiful as a dove.
It just breaks all hearts,
But I can't stop all the darts.
Why is everyone picking on me?
Can't they stop and let me be?
Hate's colours are red and black,
Love is something that I lack.
Let me be free, free from this hate,
Have I missed the love bus, am I late?
Let me be free, let me be,
Can I have the love that I can't see?

Bhavina Rana (13)
Perry Beeches School

Education Of Life

When my life comes to its end,
My spirit then will ascend.
To the place from whence I came,
To return and start again.

With life's teachings,
With falls and sorrow.
Will I learn
In life's tomorrow.

Have I learnt
From life's good will?
To take life
And my spirit fill.

My education of life is clear,
To fill my soul and spirit dear.

Paul Evans (13)
Perry Beeches School

I Hate This Life

I hate this life
She always gets the knife
And puts it against my throat
She's always beating me
I'm never allowed out
She never feeds me
I'll never be free.

I hate this life
I have no friends
No one to turn to
Nowhere to go.

I hate this life
She's always picking on me
She keeps on hurting me
She never leaves me alone
She always speaks to me with a tone
Thanks to her my clothes are all torn
I can't stand it anymore
I wish I had never been born.

Rosemerry Desouza (14)
Perry Beeches School

The Girl In The Mirror

The morn I argued with the girl in the mirror.
People say she looks just like me,
But she doesn't - I know who I am.
I swore at her, stuck up my fingers
For she gets on my nerves posing for me.
She swears back, a hot little temper she must have.
I give her an evil stare, but she stares right back -
She never flinches. She's in a world just like mine
Yet hers is better, prettier like her.
I know I don't look like her,
I know I'm rotten inside, she's perfect.
But yet not so, I'll never put my finger on it.
I peek round the edge of the mirror, she follows suit,
Curious at why she lurks the other side of my mirror.
I reach out my hand, as does she,
Only to touch cold glass. In our eyes,
A look begging to be given the answer to this mystery.
Two girls so the same, yet I know we're not.
Always battling, getting nowhere.
Someone whispers in my ear a single, obviously untrue, word:
Vanity.

Helen Bragger (13)
Queen Mary's High School

Stormy Night

Crashing, banging, lightning strikes
Scaring children, giving them frights,
Pitter-patter, howling wind
Sounding like an evil thing,
Then in the morning, when it's all died down,
The sun is shining all around.

Rachel Frosdick (11)
Sutton Coldfield Grammar School for Girls

Cats

Cats, what are they?
Long, fluffy animals,
Playful, joyful animals,
Bumpy, jumpy animals.

Cats, how do they feel?
Just like a ball of wool,
Smooth and silky,
Fluffy and soft.

Cats, how do they look?
Sweet and innocent,
Kind and generous,
Lovely and mischievous.

Cats, what do they see?
They see things through their luminous eyes,
They see their yummy food in their dish,
They see their brothers and sisters
And most of all, they see you!

Jamini Patel (11)
Sutton Coldfield Grammar School for Girls

Simile Poem

Leaping like frogs in the sun,
Soft as new silk and glistening like diamonds,
Playing like children, having fun,
Squeaky like an oily door,
Shaped like a crescent moon in the night sky,
Sweet and as gentle as rain,

A . . . dolphin.

Rebekah Chamberlain (11)
Sutton Coldfield Grammar School for Girls

Sherbet Lemons

As I open the wrapper
My hands shaking with anticipation
I smell the citric lemon flavouring.

The colour of the sweet shouts out at me,
It was as fluorescent as a highlighter.

As I open my mouth the
Sherbet lemon acts like a train
And enters a dark tunnel.

When sucking the sweet
A sensational feeling hits me,
Like a time bomb exploding
The sherbet hits the roof of my mouth
As it comes rushing out.

Amrit Lyall (11)
Sutton Coldfield Grammar School for Girls

The Black Cat

Its fur's as black as midnight.
Its claws pop out like toast from a toaster.
It creeps around the house like
A robber when they're stealing stuff.
Pink tongue looks like a blob of strawberry ice cream.
It sounds like a baby crying in a crib.
When it curls up in front of the fire it looks
Like a black ball.

Kimberley Rose (11)
Sutton Coldfield Grammar School for Girls

A Winter's Day

Biting

The ice was biting on everyone's fingers
Like a pack of wolves wanting their dinner,
Jack Frost had been up to his tricks again
Like a monkey that had stolen your hat,
Everybody was wrapped up in layers
Like presents waiting to be opened,
Feet were crunching in the snow
Like a rabbit eating lettuce.

Freezing

The wind was as sharp as a knife
Cutting through the air,
People were shaking, shivering
Like a jelly on a plate,
The snow was like a thick white blanket,
Covering everything in sight.

Snowing

The town was like a painting
Which had just been created,
The silence was like a CD player
Whose volume had been turned down low,
A winter's day is like a present,
Full of different surprises.

Charlotte Jenner (12)
Sutton Coldfield Grammar School for Girls

The Storm

Rain, like the beating of a drum.
Wind, bending the trees like gymnasts.
Lightning, as bright as the sun.
Thunder, as loud as a football ground.
The sky, as black as a blackboard,
As fierce as a pack of snarling dogs.

Eleanor Jenkins (12)
Sutton Coldfield Grammar School for Girls

Ambulance

An ambulance hurries like
Ants collecting seeds.
The ambulance is as green as grass
And as yellow as busy bees.
The ambulance is as
Hard as a rock.
The horn sounds as loud
As a scream.
It sounds like thunder.
The lights flash like
Lightning on a cold, dark night.
Ambulances go back and forth
Like a big roller coaster.

Sumita Patel (12)
Sutton Coldfield Grammar School for Girls

Bananas

The banana is as curly as my sister's hair,
It is as yellow as the shining sun at midday.
The taste is as sweet as crystal sugar.
When you hold it it feels like a smooth silk sari.
To peel the banana is like pulling
A box of a thousand books.
Once eaten it feels like I'm on cloud 9.
I love eating bananas as much as I like my sleep
And as much as I like my food.

Karishma Patel (12)
Sutton Coldfield Grammar School for Girls

A Girl

Her eyes
Sparkle like the stars.
Her hair
Glistens in the sun.
Her voice
Is as soft as velvet.
Her heart
Is made of gold.

Hannah Greatrex (11)
Sutton Coldfield Grammar School for Girls

The Sea

The sea, blue like a newborn baby's eyes.
The sea, the waves tumble down like great white stallions.
The sea, shushing you like a teacher shushing her manic class.
The sea, f-f-f-freezing like you're sitting on ice.
The sea, wet like a dog licking your face.
The sea, mysterious, waiting for all your secrets to be unravelled.

Robyn Bailey (11)
Sutton Coldfield Grammar School for Girls

What Is It?

Its body is like a long twisting rope,
It's as long as the China Wall,
It's as stripy as a scarf,
It slides along the ground as slippery as an eel,
It hisses like a sizzling hot saucepan,
It is a snake!

Samantha Huxley (11)
Sutton Coldfield Grammar School for Girls

As She Walked Along . . .

Her hair was like the
waves of the sea at sunset,
and her eyes sparkled
like stars of the night.

Her smile curved
like a gymnast,
and her voice was
as sweet as candy.

Her dress was as
soft as silk,
and her shoes were
as high as houses.

Sarah Ross (11)
Sutton Coldfield Grammar School for Girls

A Dolphin

As gentle as a rose
Shining like a Sunday morning,
As friendly as a kitten,
I can't believe it's just a thing.

Twisting and turning like the waves,
Gliding through the water like a bird in the sky,
Lifting in the air like a glistening arc
Going extremely high.

There is an animal in the sea,
It's a dolphin and that's what it should be.

Salmah Lashhab (12)
Sutton Coldfield Grammar School for Girls

Snow

As everybody in the town sleeps the snow settles,
It settles like a big white blanket, tucking up the town.
As the people wake the snow has already arrived,
The children kick and roll in the refreshing blanket
Not caring that it is as cold as ice.
As the sun comes out it dazzles their eyes
Like diamonds scattered on the ground.
The snowflakes start to fall like little stars.
Until it gets dark the children play
But when they wake the snow is gone,
Just as mysteriously as it came.

Katherine Cooney (11)
Sutton Coldfield Grammar School for Girls

Night-Time

Dark like a person,
Tiptoeing silently over the world.
It's frightening
Like a long black cloak,
Only the stars to comfort.

The moon mysteriously hides behind trees
Waiting to be called.
The stars twinkle like diamonds
On a frosty ice background.

Holly Wilson (11)
Sutton Coldfield Grammar School for Girls

The Ocean

Everything was peaceful,
The sea rippling as quiet as a soft whisper.
The water's as clear as crystals,
Glistening like diamonds in the sun.

The sea kisses the shore of a sandy beach,
Then slowly retreats back into the ocean,
The waves as calm and gentle as a dove,
As peaceful as a sunny day on a deserted island.

Abigail Tullett (11)
Sutton Coldfield Grammar School for Girls

Boots!

My beautiful cat with hidden claws,
We know she likes to do her chores,
Her nice white skin is soft and thin,
She knows not to do her grin,
'Cause that's my cat!

Bina Parmar (11)
Sutton Coldfield Grammar School for Girls

Home Time

The bell that rings is as loud as a horn,
When all the parents are outside they all chatter like parrots,
People are all rushing like there is no tomorrow,
Everyone forgets homework like they have holes in their heads,
The car park is as busy as a theme park,
Then everyone goes and it's like a ghost town.

Alice Chester (11)
Sutton Coldfield Grammar School for Girls

Dolphins

The dolphin is as gentle as a dove
Swimming gracefully through the undisturbed, blue ocean.
As it does its somersaults
It looks as proud as a peacock
And also as happy as a lark.

The water on the dolphin's back sparkles like stars
And the sun shines like diamonds
On the calm, crystal clear water.
As dusk approaches
The dolphin swims swiftly towards the sunset.

Serena Varma (11)
Sutton Coldfield Grammar School for Girls

What Am I?

As graceful as a ballerina
Though it is like a prisoner - trapped,
Being magnified, as though under inspection.
As colourful as rays of light shining
Through the peaceful countryside.

Answer - a goldfish in a bowl.

Rebecca Tancred (11)
Sutton Coldfield Grammar School for Girls

The City

The morning dawns,
The smoke creeps,
Covers the city like a grey sheet.

The cars come out
Onto the black leather,
Slithering like snakes through the thick weather.

The gutter's full of rubbish,
The drains overflow
Full of green gunk, melting like snow.

The newspapers dawdle
Along the grey streets,
Their hands in their pockets, dragging their feet.

Philippa Skett (11)
Sutton Coldfield Grammar School for Girls

The Night Before Christmas

The rooftops look like snowballs,
The trees are covered in lights,
Everyone's sleeping like a hedgehog,
As quiet as a mouse.

The front room's all quiet
As everyone's in bed,
Until Santa pops down the chimney
And gives the cat a fright.

Amy Evans (12)
Sutton Coldfield Grammar School for Girls

A Party

Colourful like traffic lights, forever changing,
As noisy as a pack of wolves,
No room for the sound of the cat whimpering for food.

Everyone was as drunk as ever,
But spirits were still as high as a kite,
But some people were just mad like monkeys.

The walls were glistening like diamonds,
The room was like a giant tomato
With light shining on it.

Jodie Tatlow (11)
Sutton Coldfield Grammar School for Girls

Snow

It twists round everything like a whirlwind,
It covers everything like a blanket.
As you wave your feet crunch like teeth.
It's as slippery as butter,
It's as white as fresh, clean paper
And it's as fun as opening presents on Christmas Day.

Lucy Sabell (11)
Sutton Coldfield Grammar School for Girls

What Is It?

It calls like a blowing whistle,
It jumps as high as Mount Everest,
It swims as swiftly as a swooping bird,
It is as friendly as a true friend,
It is as quiet as a mouse,
It has a nose as long as a bottle,
It is as grey as a stormy sky,
It swims in packs like sharks,
It is as talented as an orchestra,
Its name is a bottle-nosed dolphin.

Ruth Askey (11)
Sutton Coldfield Grammar School for Girls

The Dragon

The golden scales glistening in the sunlight,
The silver teeth sparkling in the moonlight,
The onyx claws as smooth as glass,
The scaly wings folded against the plated back,
The golden dragon basking in all its glory,
Truly this is a sight to behold.

The purifying fire shooting out of the wide mouth,
The crimson flame scorching all before it,
None survive the heat of dragon flame,
Few can even stand before the might of the dragon,
And fewer still can stand without quaking with terror,
But even in all its rage
The golden dragon is truly a sight to behold.

Michael Justice (15)
Windsor High School

Is The Body A Machine?

Our bodies work like well-tuned clocks,
To start it off there's building blocks,
Bits and bobs complete our frame,
Everybody needs the same.

But when it comes down to it all
Our genes decide if we are tall,
Brown hair, blonde hair, genes make the choice,
Right down to the sound of our voice.

So when our bodies feel the pain,
Can feel the wet drip from the rain
And cry and laugh and fall in love,
Be happy, sad, live like a dove.

It can't be made or manufactured,
The feelings come from deep inside.
So yes, our frame is the machine
And our feelings will be seen.

But, to live with no emotion or desire
Our bodies will just be machines.

Vanessa Johnson (14)
Windsor High School

The Magic Of Books

I finished the book and felt their loss,
So deep it had touched me I wept in silence
As I had read the last pages of the story,
Racked with tension, the real world drifted away.
I lay so still in my bed, that I felt nothing,
Not even the subconscious turning of the page.
No sound penetrated this new world in which I was engrossed,
At least none of the ones that existed around the real me.
Like a ghost I watched the story unfold,
Yet even as a ghost I could feel.
And when they felt sadness, I felt it too;
And then their hearts would overflow with joy and happiness,
As would mine;
And my heart fluttered with theirs as they realised their love;
And my tears wet the pages as they cried in the night.
My world was gone as I continued to read.
Had I wanted to stop, I'm not sure I could have done.
Even now, long after it ended,
I still feel the emotions that came to me then.

Hannah Beddard (14)
Wolverhampton Girls' High School

Friendship - A Special Gift

Friendship is sincerity wrapped in a smile,
A corner of tenderness shared for a while.

A milestone that brightens each step of the way,
Like a beautiful thought at the start of the day.

Friendship is the most precious gift one can hold,
It cannot be purchased with mountains of gold.

It's a hand on the shoulder when problems increase,
Knowing that soon all your troubles will cease.

It's being protective when hope tumbles down,
A fault that's forgiven, a smile for a frown.

Encouragement offered when the going is rough,
It's a hand set to help when the job is too tough.

Friendship is the essence of faith, deep and strong,
Someone to be there when things are going wrong.

It's a niche in the heart that is suddenly filled,
A deep-seated longing discovered and stilled.

A sharing of laughter, a heart filled with pleasure,
A good-natured friend is the rarest of treasure.

Davinder Kaur (16)
Wolverhampton Girls' High School

God's Gift To Mankind

There is peace in the air as dawn is breaking,
Light scatters the land as the world is awaking.

The branches are swaying in the soft breeze,
The birds are singing on the tops of the trees.

The mountains are covered with snow, like a white sheen,
The hills are specked with many shades of green.

Colourful flowers can be seen everywhere,
Their sweet-smelling fragrances spread through the air.

The sun's rays on the water make it ripple and shine,
The golden gleams on the sand make it more divine.

The tide comes in bringing with it lots of treasure,
Finding rare and pretty things fills one with pleasure.

There is peace in the air as the sun goes down,
The stars light the sky like jewels in a crown.

This unique place reflects the beauty of nature,
Making one thankful to the Almighty Creator.

Harpreet Kaur (13)
Wolverhampton Girls' High School

Flowers, A Girl's Best Friend

A dog is a man's best friend,
Flowers are mine,
Pretty as a picture,
Made to shine.

A buttercup's yellow like a golden sun
Whereas a rose is red and unique.
Ivy surrounds a house,
Flowers are divine, yes I'm a flower freak.

Daisies blossom in white and yellow,
Bluebells bloom in blue,
Pansies are a rainbow of colour,
I bet a flower show gets quite a queue.

So there you have it
From flower to flower,
Their colours and types
With their wicked power.

Chelsea Jarvis (11)
Woodway Park School

Seven Deadly Sins

Lust, to lust for sex from another.
Greed, to have money one way or another.
Pride, to be wanted by one's greatness.
Envy, to hate someone with hatred.
Wrath, to get angry out of spite.
Sloth, to be lazy out of sight.
Gluttony, to have what you want all the time.

> These are the seven deadly sins,
> Be careful as if
> You commit just
> One your life
> Is in ruins!

Jade Treadwell (15)
Woodway Park School

The Beach

The calm sea creeps up the smooth sand
As the fish swim for a place to sleep the night.
Hear the gentle waves lapping against the sharp rocks.

It's morning again and the sun is shining,
The fish come out to play.
The crabs come out from under the shells,
The palm trees sway in the calm wind.

The adults sit watching their children
As they play happily in the glittering sea.
The donkeys plod around
As they give children donkey rides.

The sun has started to set
But it isn't night-time yet.
People are starting to clear the beach.

The sun has said goodbye again,
Now the stars are glittering in the dark sky.
The fish are going back home.

Danielle Keith (11)
Woodway Park School

How I Feel

I love you more than words can say,
I can't explain how I feel,
It is so surreal,
Whenever we're apart
It breaks my china heart,
Whenever we're together
I feel I could hold you forever.

Joe Greenway (15)
Woodway Park School

What Is It?

Can you feel the cold, wet feeling
Running down your spine?
I can.
Do you hear the whispering in your
Ears day and night?
I can.
Sometimes do you think there's something supernatural
In the same room as you?
I do.
Is there times when you feel scared and lonely?
I do.
Do you see that thing behind you running, jumping,
Waiting for the right moment to leap out and grab you?
I did.
Are you in a place where there's no exit, no turning back,
Up high in the sky waiting for another chance to live?
I am, I am.

Blake Smith (11)
Woodway Park School

Happiness

Tears running down your face,
As they slip into your mouth,
A sea is replaced,
Open spaces, water all around
With no one's hands
To hold you when you are down,
To pick you up off the ground,
To love you so you hide your frown.

Rebecca Mason (15)
Woodway Park School

The Sun

The immense sun
Demolishing the darkness,
Giving light to the universe,
Overpowering the minuscule planets surrounding it,
The ferocious fiery ball of gas in the cat-black sky,
Do not look,
Do not approach,
Ever shrinking, our life force will die, and so will we,
The sun's enormous gravitational force
Pulling us ever closer,
Will this extremely bright star not eventually burn us all
Or will it die before we get that close?
Burn or freeze?
No one knows,
No one wants to know.

Zak Baldwin (11)
Woodway Park School

Love And Loss

How I miss your gentle touch
And the way you held me tight,
And when I was asleep in bed
The way you'd kiss me goodnight.
I miss the way you held my hand
When walking down the street,
And when you were around me
My heart would skip a beat.
Words can never explain
How much I miss your smile,
And how we were only together
For a short - yet wonderful while.
In bed, alone, I lay,
Missing you more and more each day.

Bonnie Gregory (13)
Woodway Park School

When I Am Dead

When I am dead
I don't want any tears for me,
No sadness or darkness,
My love will always be.
I'll think of you every day,
You'll always be here with me
No matter what you say.

I don't want any dark colours
Or sad songs played for me,
Be yourself so I can remember
The way you used to be.
I want you to be happy
And I don't want pain for me,
I'll love you forever and ever
And that's how it's to be.

Holly Dunn (13)
Woodway Park School

Death

Death is pain.
Death is a dream world
Which you fall into.
It is a cry for
Many families' hearts
As it is sometimes justice
To be paid.
On death's door people
Lie till they die
A painful death.
Life is a long thing,
Death is a short thing.
Families' sorrow is as long as they want
But the spirit is forever.

Aaron Anderson (13)
Woodway Park School

Don't Look At Me

Do you think I like it when you stand there and stare
Because I am different,
Because I have strange hair?

Do you think I like it when you call me names
Because I am alone,
Because I don't play your games?

Do you think I like it when you throw things at me
Because I am ugly,
Because I don't look like you?

Well now I don't care
If you don't like my hair.
I don't care if you call me names
Because I don't play your games.
And I don't care if you throw things at me
Because I am ugly.

Because I have learnt to ignore you
And know that it's what's inside that counts,
So here right now I'll get on one knee
And shout out to the world don't look at me.

Georga Wright
Woodway Park School

I Need To Escape

I need to escape,
It's torture in here.
There's no sunlight,
I cry every night.

I need to escape,
It's torture in here.
I work every day
For a whip, not pay.

I need to escape,
It's torture in here.
I miss my mum and dad,
It makes me very sad.

I need to escape,
It's torture in here.
And one day I do,
God Almighty - thank you.

Kieran Armour   (12)
Woodway Park School

The Ghost

It glides through the wall in the dead of night
Shimmering silver, translucent white,
It's ghosts.

Its gaunt, rotting face howls and moans,
It must be in agony from its spooky groans,
It's ghosts.

It seeps through corridors, rooms and doors,
Its piercing scream shocks to the core,
It's ghosts.

But in this state it hates to be,
All it wishes is to be free,
The ghost.

Lisa Warwick   (16)
Woodway Park School

Our World

We live in a world that as a race we contrived
Where destruction, fear and hate can thrive.

We live in a world where power conceals truth
And there is little tolerance for wisdom or youth.

We live in a world where our people starve on the streets
Yet the scrounging deceivers get the rewards and the treats.

We live in a world where sick children will die
Yet no one has stopped it - although they do try.

We live in a world where as women we're second
Instructed by men to jump when we're beckoned.

We live in a world where the old shake with fear
And people only stand up for those who are dear.

We live in a world where image is all
You must be blonde, thin, superficial and tall.

Yet I live in a world full of luxury and fun
But how can I enjoy it until the suffering is done?

Claire Kelly (15)
Woodway Park School

The Bird Of The Night

She comes shining like a silver feather through the sky,
And you can hear her cry.

The sky darkens as she flies,
The people sleep and the stars awaken.

The moon peeps over a cloud
And whispers something in her ear.

She flies and calls to waken night,
She forgives all and lands feathery kisses
In the air as she glides.

Then the dawn comes and she must sleep.

Vanessa Mignanelli (12)
Woodway Park School

Justina

Oh my God there's been a fire
Justina's rolling in a tyre.

Oh my God someone's told a lie
Justina's got a pencil thrown at her eye.

Oh my God there's a sky up above,
Justina wants to know where is the love?

Oh my God I'm being followed by the paparazzi,
Justina's taking a 28" TV home in a taxi.

Oh my God that was a nasty trick,
Justina's gone to see Ryan at Frankie and Benny's with Nick.

Oh my God I smell something eggy,
Justina said it was her auntie Debbie.

Oh my God that necklace is pearl,
Justina Angus is a racquet girl.

Oh my God there's been a fight,
This poem was written by Kimberley Knight.

Kimberley Knight (15)
Woodway Park School

My Cat

She looks small and cute
With her ginger paws.
On the tree in the garden
She sharpens her claws.

She wakes me in the morning
By purring down my ear,
And when she's hungry
She miaows and makes it very clear.

Sometimes she still acts like a kitten
And runs around the house and goes mad,
But at the end of the day when she's tired
She sleeps at the bottom of my bed.

Kelly Hadland (14)
Woodway Park School

I Sit At The Window

I sit at the window,
What do I see?
A world that does not include me.

I sit at the window,
Why do I look?
To try and find what somebody took.

I sit at the window,
What's there to find?
Nothing and no one of my kind.

I sit at the window
Watching the shore,
Hoping to be whole as before.

I sit at the window,
What do I know?
That sometime, some day I'll manage to go.

I sit at the window,
What do I see?
One day I'll find a place where I can be free.

Beth Patricia Wild (15)
Woodway Park School

The Tree

The tree just stands there
Blowing in the breeze.
They are good for climbing,
They grow big and strong.
Swooping all around the place
The top might just go to space.
I wish I could grow like a tree
Or even a tree the size of me.

Thomas Lilley (12)
Woodway Park School

When We Are Apart

When we are apart
Half my body feels dead,
Can't stop all these thoughts
Flying round in my head.

I remember when you
Would just look at me smiling,
A smile saved from you
Would stop my heart crying.

I know that right now
That something feels missing,
Is it the contact,
The hugging, the kissing?

All that I know is that
Whatever this is will soon go,
And we will be back
To the good times we know.

Times when we laughed
And we joked and we played.
Times we did nothing
And still our love stayed.

When I am dead
And my bones are rotten,
Turn back to this page
To show I'm not forgotten.

Sleep safe in the knowledge
That I'll always love you!

Rebecca Lambeth (15)
Woodway Park School

It Happened To Me

I can't believe it happened to me,
You never think 'me' until it happens.
You hear about it happening to other people,
It happens to people you don't even know.
You realise it's bad when it happens to you
But you never think 'me'.

I can't believe it happened to me,
When it happens to you, you don't want to believe it.
Of all the people it happened to me,
After a while what happened sinks in.
Then you realise 'it happened to me',
Why does it have to happen to me?
What shall I do now it's happened to me?
Now I can't change what happened to me.

Samantha Mountain (15)
Woodway Park School

Pitch-Black

Suddenly, pitch-black, total darkness,
I can't see a thing in sight,
Trying to find something to bare a bit of light.

My heart starts to race,
With a lump in my throat, suddenly I'm aware,
Hoping that nothing and no one is there.

With my torch held tight by my side
I start to move,
Trying to find my way out within the room.

I come to a stop with my hand on the door handle,
I push it down,
Suddenly I see . . . I drop to the ground.

Victoria Jukes (15)
Woodway Park School

Goodbye

You made me laugh,
You made me cry,
You made me see life in a whole new way.

You took hold of my hand
And helped me
Through the bad times in life.

One day my mum told me
That you were gone.

I couldn't believe it,
The man in my life was gone,
I would never see him again.

I said goodbye to your body
But not to your soul,
As you remain in my heart every day of my life.

Grandad I loved you so much
And I always will,
Goodbye, your favourite grandaughter, Emma.

Emma Bedford (15)
Woodway Park School

Friends' Value

Some people think it's great to be rich,
To be cool and have the trends,
But do money and looks really matter?
What really matters is *friends!*

Toni-Marie Jackson (11)
Woodway Park School

Deserted House

The deserted house is dark and dingy,
Doorknobs sticky and spider webs clingy.
Broken windows, crooked doors,
Dripping pipes and creaking floors.

Mice running everywhere,
From hole to hole without a care.
Water dripping from the rusted tap,
As a huge spider drops on your lap.

You push it off and begin to think,
But you're disturbed by the sound of the kitchen sink.
You remember the murder crime,
But stop as it is full of guts and grime.

You begin to leave and pick up the pace,
As the image changes upon your face.
You're surrounded by a ghost and a ghoul,
Now you wish you hadn't bunked off school.

Now you're buried in a grave,
Some people might think that you were brave.
But the stories have changed to you,
Now you're the one to scare people through.

Nathan Allsopp (14)
Woodway Park School

I'm Alive

I'm alive but feeling like there's nothing standing
Worthy of my expectation,
A groan of tedium escapes me,
I'm stumbling so fearful,
I must keep reminding myself I'm alive.

I'm alone, so wide eyed and hopeful,
Spinning down the spiral,
I'm damned to disappear,
Is all of this real or just an illusion?
Please save me from my insane self.

And now I'm bruised and borrowed,
Feeling forsaken and rueful,
Got nothing left to give you,
So watch me as I crumble
But wake me as I fall.

Mitchel Hand (16)
Woodway Park School

Apes In Danger

I see them in the bushes,
Some swinging from tree to tree,
So many of them all looking at me.
Thinking there is danger ahead
Some people try and save them from
The dangers of the forest.

The apes are in danger,
They have come to cut down the forest for the trees.
The men have no idea of what mess they will leave.
Animals have no home when it has gone.
What a mess!

Lara Suddens (11)
Woodway Park School

Trapped In The Wake of A Dream

He was brought into the world, without consent or choice,
Born a bastard son, confused of whom his father.
Lived alone, in a broken home and never saw the point
In dreaming of reality - when he cannot live one.

Picked on in and outside of school, he drowns in his pity,
The wild, waving water making his every attempt to breathe
Sweet, innocent air, he needs it like his first love - pity.
Shame, for he cannot wake up - trapped in the wake of his dream.

He craves for his dead mother to make her return,
Ran away with a tall, dark man, left the boy to survive alone.
He only sees bitter hope, in the depth of a chamber,
Down the dark barrel of a capable killing machine.

I am that bastard son, for I was brought into this world,
The trigger promises a happy ending, a mere short cut,
I do not wish to be anymore . . .
For I am trapped in the wake of my dream.

Christopher Worsley (16)
Woodway Park School

Happiness?

Happiness. What does it mean?
Is it the smile that reassures everyone that you are alright
Or the feelings that make you cry deep in the night?
Is it everyone thinking that nothing is wrong
Or the loneliness and sadness that you've felt for so long?

Happiness. How long will it last?
Until your dreams are but a distant memory
Or until someone finally hears your silent plea?
Is it when you give up hope on human kind
Or search for the love you will never find?

Happiness. Does it really exist?

Katie Cawte (16)
Woodway Park School

My Lonely Soul

As I lie among the wilderness,
All tattered, torn and bruised
I look for inspiration,
But nothing seems to move.

A gentle breeze blows over
And it chills me to the bone,
Around me trees will rustle,
That's when I feel alone.

In the morning, as I wake,
I get up and move along,
Life don't seem so welcome
So I whistle and sing a song.

Life has got too hard
And as I lay upon my bench,
I reflect on days gone by
And it all seems such a wrench.

I don't want to live like this
And no longer see the point,
So I'll come down from my pride perch
And begin to start from scratch.

Paul Martin (14)
Woodway Park School

My Wild Dreams

I dream of . . .

           being a scientist finding cures for all diseases,
           from cancer and leukaemia to common colds
           and sneezes.

I dream of . . .

           being a rock star singing on TV
           with fans buying CDs and big posters of me.

I dream of . . .

           being a millionaire with houses, cars and boats
           and lots of clothes and jewellery
           and fancy shoes and coats.

I dream of . . .

           being an artist painting pictures by the sea,
           my paintings would be hung and sold in every gallery.

I dream of . . .

           being a teacher working in a school,
           but I wouldn't be too strict, I'd be really fun and cool.

I dream of . . .

           being happy in everything I do
           and all my wishes and my hopes
           and my dreams come true.

Chelsea Bentley (14)
Woodway Park School

September 11th

Everyone remembers that terrible day,
What they were doing, who they were with, where they were,
A day that scarred so many lives,
From all the corners of the Earth.

Those two Twin Towers standing proud and firm,
Full of hustle and bustle and wheeling and dealing.
The chatter, the laughter, the telephone calls,
A place of business and commerce left reeling.

The tragic television coverage lasted all day,
We watched anxiously as the horror unveiled.
From when the planes crashed into the sides,
To the carnage and the devastation.

Now those two proud buildings have gone for good,
The memorable skyline has changed forever.
But they were just bricks and mortar - a shell,
It's the death of the innocent people that matters.

September the 11th is a day the world will never forget,
A day that's etched on our minds and in our hearts forever.

Daniel Davis (14)
Woodway Park School

I Wish . . .

I wish I were famous,
I wish that I could fly.
I wish for peace, love and happiness,
So I wouldn't cry.
I wish I could have freedom,
I wish I could live forever,
I wish I could have you here with me
And always be together.
I wish for you and me,
I wish for me and you,
I wish, I wish, I really, really wish
That this would all come true.
But, if I could have only one wish
I'd wish for a thousand more.
But what would be the point?
You would be the one I'd keep wishing for.

Samantha Dick (14)
Woodway Park School

My Alien Friend

I have an alien friend called Zog,
He comes from a planet called Pog.
He's green with pink spots
And he eats lots and lots.
Zog likes spiders and slugs
And any type of horrible bugs.
He tells funny tales
About animals and whales.
Zog is really clever,
He can tell the future and predict the weather.
He lives with his girlfriend called Blip,
In his own funny-shaped spaceship.
Together
They'll live happily in Pog forever.

Lucy Ridding (12)
Woodway Park School

There's A Monster Under My Bed

'Mum, there's a monster under my bed.'
'Don't be silly,' my mum said.
But you know what, I'm not lying,
Let me tell you what he's like.

He's under my bed waiting for me,
He's up the walls longing to be free,
His long claws stick out like knives,
No wonder he hasn't got any wives.

His teeth are like sharp daggers
Waiting to plunge into my flesh,
And I wouldn't be surprised
If he had five eyes.

He's under my bed waiting for me,
He will not rest until I'm *dead!*

Nikita Hall (11)
Woodway Park School

Beautiful Butterflies

Butterflies - what strange
And magical creatures.
It's hard to believe they were once tiny grubs,
When you look at them now
With their delicate, fragile wings
Of all colours,
Red, blue, gold, white, yellow.
They don't seem to belong to this world,
Flitting busily from flower to flower
Enjoying the sunshine.
What a wonderful life a butterfly has,
No cares, no worries.
It's so tragic they only live a while,
But their time spent on this Earth
Is very worthwhile.

Emma Mignanelli (14)
Woodway Park School

Four Seasons

The park stands on the edge of town
Covered in a thick white blanket
Of pure, white snow.
Trees support thin, bare branches
Swaying to and fro,
To and fro . . .
The park stands on the edge of town,
Birds chirp merrily
In the dry spring breeze.
Paths are covered in blossom,
Another year, a new beginning,
A new life . . .
The park stands on the edge of town,
The sun beats down on the dry, yellow grass.
Children playing merrily on the swings,
The park is alive with sounds and noises,
People enjoying picnics and outings,
Relaxing through the long, calm evenings . . .
The park stands on the edge of town,
Autumn has finally arrived,
Paths are littered with leaves,
Green and brown, red and orange.
Lonely winds are wailing,
Creaking swings are swaying to and fro,
To and fro, calling to be wanted . . .

Kamala Mistry (14)
Woodway Park School

An Icy Cold Day!

The wind shook,
The wind blew,
It shook the plants
Where the flowers grew.

The sun shone
Although it was cool,
The bushes even moved,
Tall and small.

Daisies withered,
Brown leaves flew,
It was so quiet,
Why, nobody knew.

The breeze slowed down
And rippled through my hair,
Rustling sounds
Stayed in the air.

The hutch was icy cold,
Damp and wet,
As I leant over
I fed my cute pet.

Laura Barrett (12)
Woodway Park School

All Aboard The Ghost Train

There's a tumble-down old station
Where a ghost train waits to go,
All aboard ghosts, ghouls and goblins,
Watch the engine brightly glow.

Ghostly sounds are whistling wildly,
Bony fingers wave goodbye,
As along the rails the ghost train glides
Beneath the moonlit sky.

Witches shriek along the rail cars
While inside the dining cars
Vampires munch and crunch with monsters
Sipping cocktails at the bar.

If there were tickets for the ghost train
Would you dare to take a ride,
Or would you quickly run away
And find somewhere to hide?

    So tell me!

Katie Read (14)
Woodway Park School

Willow Tree

I sit under a willow tree,
Nothing around but little old me.
I look around to see what's to see,
But nothing around just little old me.

I sit under a willow tree,
Watching the birds as they flee.
I'm sitting here with just me,
Me and my old willow tree.

David Wild (12)
Woodway Park School